James Carnegie Southesk

The Burial of Isis

And Other Poems

James Carnegie Southesk

The Burial of Isis
And Other Poems

ISBN/EAN: 9783744712361

Printed in Europe, USA, Canada, Australia, Japan

Cover: Foto ©Thomas Meinert / pixelio.de

More available books at **www.hansebooks.com**

THE BURIAL OF ISIS

AND OTHER POEMS.

Edinburgh: Printed by Thomas and Archibald Constable

FOR

DAVID DOUGLAS.

LONDON . . . HAMILTON, ADAMS, AND CO.

CAMBRIDGE . . . . . MACMILLAN AND BOWES.

GLASGOW . . . . . . JAMES MACLEHOSE AND SONS.

THE BURIAL OF ISIS

AND OTHER POEMS

BY

THE EARL OF SOUTHESK

K.T.

EDINBURGH: DAVID DOUGLAS

1884

DEC 1 6 1966

TO

MY WIFE

I DEDICATE

THIS BOOK.

PREFACE.

THIS volume contains most of the verses comprised in *Greenwood's Farewell, and other Poems* (1876), and nearly all of those belonging to *The Meda Maiden, and other Poems* (1877); also various unpublished poems, which, with one exception, have been written since the latter date. Several of the pieces taken from the published volumes are now more or less altered; and all of them, together with the new verses, are intermingled without regard to any previous arrangements. As a matter of convenience the book has been divided into sections, partly according to subject, but under no strict rules in that respect. The reference-numbers, throughout, relate to notes in the Appendix. These are chiefly explanatory, except as regards 'The Meda Maiden,' where they furnish information on subjects only alluded to, or slightly noticed, in the poem.

As a rule the contents of this volume are objective, not subjective, in their relation to the Author. That is to say, the Author must not be understood as speaking for, or of, himself—whether the first or third person be used,—unless in certain passages, whose intention should be sufficiently clear to an impartial eye. Most of the songs and other compositions are entirely dramatic in their general design; some, perhaps, may to a certain extent express the Author's occasional feelings, and there are a few (*e.g.* 'The Rocky Mountains') that can hardly be separated from his own personality; none of these, however, are to be taken as *proprid persond* utterances, nor as revelations of secret thought or records of private adventure.

Needless statements, it may be said; but there are circumstances under which such explanations become useful, and almost necessary, as a defence against wrong; perhaps, indeed, in the present case they may be otherwise serviceable in aiding the judgment of generous readers and fair-minded critics—for whose consideration this volume is, with all respect, submitted.

CONTENTS.

PRELUDE.

PART I.

PART II.

PART III.

PART IV.

PRELUDE.

A

WINTER GLORIES.[1]

'TIS in the winter of the year,
A silent, sad November day;
The beech is brown, the oak is sere,
The ash is sallow gray.

The blackbird on the balustrade
Beside the golden-olive moss,
His morning feast has yonder made
Where crimson berries cross.

The shaggy cattle in the park
Move gently on like mystic dreams,
And o'er the herbage dun and dark
Their silvery softness gleams.

And, through the orange fern, the deer
Among the fir-trees idly stray:
The beech is brown, the oak is sere,
The fir is green alway.

NOVEMBER'S CADENCE.

THE bees about the Linden-tree,
When blithely summer blooms were springing,
Would hum a heartsome melody,
The simple baby-soul of singing:
And thus my spirit sang to me
When youth its wanton way was winging;
'Be glad, be sad—thou hast the choice—
But mingle music with thy voice.'

The linnets on the Linden-tree,
Among the leaves in autumn dying,
Are making gentle melody,
A mild, mysterious, mournful sighing:
And thus my spirit sings to me
While years are flying, flying, flying;
'Be sad, be sad—thou hast no choice—
But mourn with music in thy voice.'

NORTHERN MAY.

THE north wind blows, but the sun is bright,
The winter's snows are on the height,
And the trembling beeches scarcely dare
To show their buds to the frozen air;
Yet up on the top of the highest tree
The valiant Thrush sings loud and free.

And down in the yews so darkly green,
Whose limbs refuse their summer sheen
Lest the tender shoots should faint and die
At the touch of the tempest cold and high,
The musical Blackbird chants his lays,
And sighs not for the summer days.

Now sweetly sound the Cushat's notes,
And far around their softness floats,
And the bitter breezes grow more mild
As they carry along those wood-notes wild.
Sing heartily, birds, all fears above!
Ye sing in hope, ye sing in love.

FOREST FRAGRANCE.[2]

O YELLOW Whin in the wood!
O yellow Broom in the pines!
Your goldenness is wondrous good,
And with your scent combines
To image delicate wines.

O eyes of the life of the world!
O breaths of the world's perfume!
Small sprites lie close within you curled,
And twinkle through the Broom,
And the Whin's light illume.

SUNSET AFTER STORM.[3]

A HEAVEN of blue and silver sheen
Comes smiling in the sky;
Black mists are rolling off, between
The distant and the nigh.

And o'er the craggy eastward vale
Vast ships of vapour sweep,
And soar away with golden sail
Above the mountain steep.

PART I.

THE BURIAL OF ISIS.[4]

THEY carried it far by wood and wold,
  And away by the water's flow,
To the gray old stone that stands alone
Where the oaks are broad and low.

And they looked around to the heathy moor,
And they looked to the greenwood bowers,
And they looked to the dell, where the wild-boar's
    snout
Had scattered the primrose flowers.

And one of them searched by the winding brook,
And one of them climbed a tree;
Save the curlew's cry they nothing heard,
And never a thing did see.

Then they went to the foot of the tall gray stone—
The young man and the old,—
And they opened a bundle of gray wolf-skins,
And many a length unrolled.

And therein was a figure small, of stone—
A woman, black to see,—
And all bare she sat with a crown on her head,
And an infant on her knee.

Then to his son the father said—
His beard was long and gray—
When I was a boy I was stout of heart,
And I wandered far away.

Away from the heath and the wood and wold,
Away from Alban far;[4]
And I sailed to the South in a goodly boat,
To a land where Britons are.

They had houses made of carven stones,
They had garments soft and fine,
They had silver much and chains of gold,
And wondrous herds of kine.

For there had the wealthy warriors dwelt—
The lordly men of Rome,—
But the last of them all had sailed away
To seek for another home.

And their store they left to the men of the land,
With arms and armour bright;
'Twas an idle boon for peaceful slaves
Who had no skill to fight!

We beached our boats in a sandy bay,
And over the land we flew;
We dragged the women off in droves,
The men and babes we slew.

And we took their swords of the metal keen,
Their spears and their darts and bows;
But I held to my axe of the good gray stone
That smote such weighty blows.

Now near to the bay where we beached our boats
Were houses strong and great,
With walls around exceeding high
And a mighty brazen gate.

Then said the chief of the Cruithnê men,[4]
From Erin's isle that came,
'There is store behind that brazen door,
To leave it there were shame.'

So we hewed down trees, and we made a screen
With a roof of raw ox-hide,
And we drave it close to the brazen gate
And sheltered us inside,

Till we burst the gate with a beam of oak
And rushed upon the foe ;
Our foremost men they speared with spears,
But soon we laid them low,

And over the living and over the dead
We went like a winter's tide ;
And some went hither and some went thither :
But two of us turned aside

To a white stone house that shone in the sun,
And we burst its door of wood,
And we entered a chamber long and low ;
And there a Briton stood—

A noble youth,—and his breast and arms
With broad gold chains were spread,
An iron lance in his hand he bore
And a helm was on his head.

He drave his lance at the Cruithnê man,
Who passed me with a bound,
But ere ever the iron touched its mark
I dashed him to the ground.

Then I stooped me down for his golden chains,
And the Cruithnê man went by;
I followed him hard to the chamber's end,
For swiftly he drew nigh

To a maid who knelt upon her knees,
And with both her arms she pressed
An image of stone that was small and black,
And held it to her breast.

Her robe, as white as the downy swan,
With gold was girded fair;
Then the Cruithnê caught her by the throat
And dragged her by her hair.

But I said, 'Let be! the maid is mine;
It is thus that thou shalt pay
The debt for thy life; be thine likewise
The gold I won to-day.'

But he roared in his wrath, and he turned about
To strike me with a dart;
So I scattered his brains with my axe of stone
And clove him to his heart.

Then I lifted the maid, and I bore her off
To the boats in the sandy bay;
And I brought her safe to Alban's shore;
And I carried her far away,

Across the moor and the wood and wold,
To where I wont to dwell.
And there she lived for a year and a day;
In truth I liked her well—

Though her strength was small for the weighty work,
And few were the words she spake,
And she looked like the lights on moveless meres,
That neither sleep nor wake.

She would sit and gaze with her yearning eyes,
For a whole long summer's day,
At the small black image she held so close
When I carried her far away.

'Twas a moon before the fall of the leaf
That she bore me a living child;
I laid it gently near her breast;
She looked at it, and smiled-

The only smile that her lips had smiled
Since I brought her over the main;
Then she sank to rest with the babe on her breast,
And never breathed again.

So we carried her forth to the old gray stone,
And there her grave did make;
And the small black image she loved so well,
I kept it for her sake.

* * * * *

We reared the child, and it grew apace
A maiden tall and fair;
Her eyes were as gray as Ainè's well,[4]
And golden was her hair.

But her mother's hair was as black as a night
Where the gray old oak-trees stand;
For she sprang from a race of ancient fame,
In the far-off Roman land.

Now when years had passed, the chief of the priests,
Talurchan[4]—none could claim
A mightier power in the land than he—
To seek my dwelling came.

And he straightway said, 'Thy daughter fair
I pray thee give to me,
And to thee will I give a princely gift.'
Said I, 'This cannot be,

For a vow have I vowed at the pillar stones,
To a chief of the men of Clyde,
That to him will I give my daughter fair.'
Said he, 'Then woe betide

'Both thee and that man. Thy daughter fair
With power will I bear away;
And nor thee nor the men of all Strath-Clyde[4]
Shall dare to say me nay.'

Thereafter the feast of the Sun drew nigh;
Then the priests of the Sacred Fire
Six maidens fair for their gods did claim,
To turn them from their ire

For the Men of the West[4] had stricken us sore,
And forced us from the plain,
And the best of our kine they had driven away,
And warriors many slain.

So the Druids met at the pillar stones,
And they cast the fateful rods,
And Talurchan judged, and he claimed my child
To offer to the gods.

Then up spake the King, before us all,
In a loud and lordly voice,
'Be glad; the gods have brought thy name
Great glory by their choice.'

But he turned him round, and with a sign
He bade me to draw nigh;
'Watch well,' said he, 'and stand by me;
Thy daughter shall not die.'

Now no man heard save myself alone
That saying of the King,
For the priests were singing the sacred songs,
And loudly did they sing.

And the maidens stood at the altar-stone;
There were some that wept and sighed,
But my daughter looked like the moon in heaven
At a quiet eventide.

Around and around the Druids moved,
Till their chant was nearly done;
Then Talurchan went to the altar-stone
And raised his knife to the sun.

But behold there came forth a tall gray man
And stood by the altar-stone;
And he cried aloud, 'O evil priests,
Lo, I am here alone

'In the place of your power; but I fear ye not,
Ye false and cruel band,
For the Great God's word is in my mouth,
His might is in my hand.'

Then he spake to the people; 'Ye fools and blind,
The gods whom ye serve this day
They are thieving wolves, who rend your kine
And on your children prey.

'Are they better to you than the Men of the West,
Who crush you in their might,
Who seize your cattle and take your gold,
And slay your sons in fight?

'Yet never of old did the Western men
Withstand your strength and pride;
But they worship now the God of Heaven,
And he battles at their side.

'And that god he taketh not gold nor kine,
Nor doth their children slay,
Though he glory giveth, and strength, to those
Who love him and obey.
Now hearken well, O Men of the East,
And turn to him this day.'

While he spake a power was laid on all,
And the priests stood silent by;
But when that he ceased Talurchan said,
'This man shall surely die.'

And he thrust with his knife at the tall gray man;
But, swiftly as he sped,
The King struck first with his iron sword
And clove Talurchan's head.

Then some of the chiefs stept forth, and smote
The Druids as they ran ;
And many were slain, but the most were spared
At the voice of the tall gray man,

Saying, 'Hold ye your hands, and hearken all ;
Let no more bloodshed be ;
For my god he seeketh not for blood.'
Then to the King said he,

'Right well hast thou done the will of God ;
Now wherefore doubting stay ?
But turn with thy heart to the living God,
To be thy god this day.'

So the King, and the chiefs, and the warriors all
Went down to the Druids' lake,
And the man in gray on their brows that day
The sign of Christ did make.

Then it came to pass that the Men of the West
Sent gold and droves of kine,
And they said to the King, 'Let fighting cease,
For lo, our God is thine.

'Ye shall dwell in our land as brethren dwell;
Return ye to the plain;
And with us shall ye smite the robber bands
That roam upon the main.'

So we made a league with the Western Men,
And rich in goods we grew;
And the priests of Christ they were mild and meek
While yet their rule was new.

* * * * *

The old man ceased, and a frown like night
Came over his wrinkled brow.
Then the young man said, 'Of a truth the priests
Are proud and greedy now.'

Said his father,—Since ever the shaveling priests
Were brought from across the sea,
There is neither love in the land, nor peace;
Nor e'er again shall be,

Till we mete them the measure King Urgust[4] gave
Talurchan and his crew.
Enough of words—let the work be done
That need there is to do.

For if Priest Johannes should come to spy—
As come full soon he must—
And his eyes should fall on this image small,
He would grind it into dust.

And me and thee and the whole of my house
Beneath his curse would lie;
We should live our lives in shame and dread,
And like to dogs should die.

For the very King would he blight with a ban,
Should he dare to hide and hold
The least of the things that pertain to the gods
Whom the people served of old.

Now this is the goddess-queen of Heaven,
In glory on her throne:—
So dig a hole, and bury her deep
Beneath the old gray stone.

Deep, deep they dug by the tall gray stone,
And nor halt nor pause they made
Till the father had bared the burial cell
Where his Roman wife was laid.

And there were her bones, so pure and slight
And shapely, resting there;
And around her delicate skull were spread
Her dusky locks of hair.

Then the old man lifted the image black,
And laid it near her head;
And thrice did he kiss her long soft locks,
As sudden tears he shed.

So the image small of the Queen of Heaven
Among the soft locks lay;
Then the old man closed the burial cell
And hid it from the day.

And they shovelled the sand and gravel down,
Till the pit was no more seen;
And they flattened the heap and smoothed the turf,
Till all looked fair and green.

Then away they went by the wood and wold,
And away by the water's flow,
Away from the grave at the old gray stone,
Where the oaks are broad and low.

COMPLETE AND INCOMPLETE.

STATELY in a German town—
Famous Frankfort, free no more—
Stands a tower of pointed crown
Flanked by pointed turrets four;
Tall and round and gray and great,
Guardian of an ancient gate.

Through the archway's vaulted road
Pleasant gardens meet the eye,
Set where moated waters flowed
Deeply in the days gone by;
Where the waters once were seen,
Fair are flowers and grass is green.

Joyful in the summer skies
Swifts are shrieking on their way,
Storks benignly supervise
Many a home where mortals stay,
Soaring slow, or poised at rest
Near the young ones in the nest.

Underneath a sycamore
Waits a flaxen-headed child,
Heedful of his simple store
In an open basket piled—
Store of things for humble use,
Such as peasant toils produce.

Now a carriage near him rolls,
Whirling through the shaded street,
Tender-natured kindly souls,
Lovers of the pure and sweet;
Seeing him they smiled, and said,
'Blessings on his round white head!'

With an answering smile, the boy
Stoops, and raises from the ground—
All his features lit with joy—
Something cage-like, wired around:
Holds it up, and shows a sight
Almost more than beauty bright.

Nestling near together, glow
Creatures of ethereal guise—
Small twin rabbits, white as snow,
Balas rubies are their eyes:
Soft delicious things indeed,
Sweet as lilies in a mead.

Then a flash of influence passed
(Such as from enchanter's wand
O'er a neophyte is cast),
Binding in a magic bond—
Spirit-bond that none can mar—
These who commune from afar:

Linking for a moment's space,
Soul to soul and heart to heart,
These so different of race,
These in rank so far apart,—
Sharers in a golden dream
Wafted from the Love Supreme.

Marvellous it is, and good,
All the lore by instinct taught,
Rich in secrets that elude
Wisdom's strong and steady thought
See, a peasant boy can know
More than science serves to show.

Surely an æsthetic child!
Dallying with a dainty spell,
Masterful in movement mild
Over souls that meet it well,—
Spell by Nature deftly thrown
Soon as lovely things are shown.

Things of earth, or air, or sea,
Beauteously by Nature planned;
Lovely things, whate'er they be,
Fashioned by the human hand;
These are mighty to control
Secret senses of the soul.

While the spirit (deep within,
Heavenly flame,) is all of heaven,
Soul is unto body kin,
Each by other's force is given
Impulses of boundless might,
Thrills of anguish or delight.

So the loveliness that wears
Earth's own beauty all complete,
Comes most potently, and snares
Soul and body as they meet:
Nought on earth completeness shows,
Where the spirit works and glows.

Chiefest then in earthly sway
Stand the things of nether grade,
Perfected to serve their day,
Means whereby are most displayed
Nature's potency, which lurks
Weightiest in her feebler works.

Thus the godlike human form
Fails to bid the gazer weep
Rapturous tear-drops, wandering warm
Through the central depths that sleep
Shrouded in the soul of man—
Soul-abysses hard to scan.

Yea, the majesty that dwells
Blent with hero-forms of fame,
Yea, the loveliness that swells
Softly o'er a woman's frame,
Glad the mind and carnal eyes,
Not the sense that inmost lies.

(Man is as the crawling things
Ere their loftier life accrues,
Waiting to receive their wings,
Fairer forms, and tenderer hues,—
Brightly banded, ringed, or starred,
Yet by incompleteness marred;

While the buoyant butterflies,
Brethren to the light and air,
Float enraptured in the skies,
All-complete and heavenly fair:
Simile for ever true,
Old to-day, to-morrow new.)

But the love that lives in flowers,
Insects of a gentle grace,
Birds, and creatures poor in powers,
Soft, and small, and meek of face—
Dormouse with the tiny feet,
Lily, moth, or robin sweet,—

Moulds them with all-perfectness,
Nought too much, nor aught to crave,
Makes them symbols to express
Goods that lie beyond this grave—
Grave of glory—man's old earth,
Heaped o'er seeds awaiting birth.

* * * * *

Shall we therefore chiefest prize
Lesser things, because complete?
Laud the lily, but despise
Woman's imperfection sweet?
Love the lowliness full-blown,
Scorn the nobleness half-grown?

Ah, not so! Behold them both
Glorious in their diverse ways.
Laud and love them, never loth
All things beautiful to praise:
Evermore let love go free,
Lauding all things fair to see.

Whence the old, insensate strife,
Chilling Art with breathings bleak: —
Outward form, or inward life?
Gothic soul, or body Greek?
Which shall mount the despot's throne,
There to tyrannise alone?

Whence the shallowness that spurns
Him whose brooding spirit sees —
Joys in, o'er it weeps and yearns —
Loveliness in rocks, and trees,
Mountains, and the small, sweet things
Moving there on feet or wings?

He who loveth bird or flower,
Loveth that wherein have place
Selfsame subtleties of power,
Nobleness, and nameless grace,
In their essence, as contain
Grecian statue, vase, or fane.

Samples are they, set to show
Genius, human or divine,
Lording it in regions low
Where the sensuous moonbeams shine,
Gathering glories from a store
Earthly all, nor asking more.

Mark the majesties of art
Palaced in the marble cold
Taught by Phidias to impart
Holiest Hellene dreams of old,—
Breathes there man whose wisdom dare
Change one line created there?

Not more lightly mark the charms
Nature's lowlier work displays—
Jewels for her godlike arms,
Fashioned in her idler days,
Objects of a finite grace,
Wrought to serve an Æon's space.

Look upon the finches bright
Bathing in the noon of day—
Green and golden, pink and white—
Lavishing the silvery spray:
Wouldst thou change one feather fair,
Change a line created there?

View the dormouse, in the wood
Where no sound of evil jars,
Soft as fruitage ripe for food,
Golden, eyed with ebon stars:
Wouldst thou change the tiniest hair,
Tint, or line created there?

See the roe of slender limbs,
Through the bowery bushes creep;
See the swallow, as it skims
Lightly as the sunbeams leap:
Wouldst thou change those forms of air,
Change a line created there?

Yet, of loveliest Women, none—
Though by Heaven so nobly made--
Shineth as a perfect sun
Sullied not by touch of shade,
Shadow of some thought undue,
Shadow of some forms untrue!

Heavenly are the lights that stay
Homed within a woman's eyes—
Midnight-black or morning-gray,
Ocean-green, or blue as skies;
Yet these heavenly lights proclaim
Hidden fires that waste the frame.

Spiritual potent fires
All too strong for earth to hold,
Fraught with fervour that aspires
Yearningly to realms of gold;
Regions where, in deathless sheen,
Perfect human forms are seen.

Wrought of purest light are they,
Blent in paradisal air,
More than mortal tongue can say
Lustrous and for ever fair;
High in heavenly homes they shine,
Mirrors of the light divine.

There no baleful cares are known,
There unknown is nervous blight,
All the limpid soul is seen
Luminous in lovely light;
All the form, of radiance kin,
Manifests the soul within.

There, all-perfect and complete,
Image of God's primal thought,
Man subsists in figure meet;
Nobler far than figures wrought
Broodingly by mortal skill,
Beauteous in the marble chill.

Perfect, truly, such may be,
Perfect of a lower type,
(E'en as fruitage on a tree
When its crudeness comes to ripe,)
Meet to satisfy a mind
Earthward bent and heavenward blind.

But all-perfectness in forms
Here upon this embryo earth,
Speaks of calm too free from storms,
Argues spiritual dearth,
Marks them lowly made, to blend
Earth with earth, and doomed to end.

Imperfection upward strives;
Objects that imperfect seem
Prophesy majestic lives
Following that wherewith they dream:
Body marred and soul at strife,
Mortal man but dreams in life.

* * * * *

Dreams he wisely who would bind
Art to one fair dream alone;
Painting, poesy confined
'Neath the sensuous radiance thrown
Mildly by the moon that flings
Beauty over earthly things?

Nay, he doeth well to turn
Ofttimes to the clearer light,
Issuing from the flames that burn
Coldly on Truth's altar bright:—
Dream in Beauty's radiance fair,
Wake in Truth's transcendent air!

Love the dormouse and the flower,
Love the gentle things that fly;
Love the kingly works of power,
Queenly grace, and symmetry,
Wrought by wonder-working hands
Trained in bounteous Southern lands.

Yet remember thou to love
Holier art of Northern birth,
Art that draws from realms above
Spirit-nurture strange to earth:
More than Aphroditê's grace
Dwells in 'Melencolia's' face.[5]

There as in a glass we see,
Demonised by Magian spell,
Glimpses of eternity,
Hieroglyphs that seem to tell
Mournful tidings, corpse-like cold,
Carried down from chaos old.

All the burden of the cares
Since this planet was begun;
All the load of sighs and prayers
Garnered underneath the sun;
All the ghastly groans of earth
Travailing in spirit birth;

All the long, laborious thought;
All the purgatorial fire
Forging the redemption wrought
Strong for spirits that aspire;—
All the woes of earth, complete,
Mourning in that visage meet.

Yea, moreover, in that face
Farther marvels man may view,
On its dusky features trace
Gleamings of a heavenly hue,—
Splendent glory, which appears
Rainbow'd on a cloud of tears.

Woe is the divinest thing
Moving in this world of ours,
God's own messenger to bring
Higher gifts and loftier powers;
Woe is the inspiring breath
Wafted from the angel Death.

Likewise Joy is fair and good,
Breathing on a soul at rest,—
Heaven's high purpose understood,
Perfect patience in the breast:
Earth's poor angel; Sensuous Joy,
Dances deathward—fortune's toy.

—Thus great Durer's work conveys
Truth, to holiest spirits known;
Thus the Hellenist displays
Beauty, of this earth alone:
High-imperfect, low-complete,
Both of them our love shall greet.

Endless is the world of art:
Fellow-mortals! love, I pray,
Beauty with your joyous heart;
Spurn not therefore Truth away:
Love the lovely, all above;
All things lovely deem that love.

THE WANDERER OF CLOVA.

A TRUE STORY OF 1859.

FAR from the stir of men
Lies Clova's lonely glen,
Tracked by the gray South-Esk meandering tow'rds the [seas;
On either hand are seen
Vast walls of living green,
Spotted with crags that mar their verdant harmonies.

And where the winter sun,
His short day's journey done,
Behind Tombûie's mass betakes him to the night,—
Thence started on its course,
White-Water brings its force
To meet the half-grown Esk in rivalry of might.

Adown the deep Glen Dole
Its foamy torrents roll,
With speed that scarce will grant a moment's breathing [pause,—
Still writhing at the stir
Of terror's urgent spur,
Escaping from the gripe of Luncart's rock-fanged jaws.

But ere the river raves
Through those terrific graves,
It walks with gentler step down lengths of silent vale;
A place most desolate,
High, bare, flat, formless, straight,—
All black and pallid green, hued like a dragon's mail.

Is there one earthly spot
Wherein existeth not
Some charm to win the love of things with life endued?
E'en o'er this upland grim
Aye floats Wild Nature's hymn—
That joy which praises God for solemn solitude.

'Twas in the month of June—
Sweet month that flies too soon!
When light the longest lies on this dark land of ours;
When redolent of glee
Are earth and air and sea,
And all Creation's force expands itself in flowers.

It was that season fair:
Behold, with pondering air,
Two foresters regard the lonesome upland glen—
Hearts without guile or fear,
The guardians of the deer
'Gainst hurt from stealthy act of lawless graceless men.

Silent they sat, and eyed
Tombûie's sallow side,
And scanned the Corrie's rocks, in many a splinter thrown:
When sudden, in surprise,
One to the other cries :—
'What, what is that I see beside yon great gray stone?'

'Twas a mere strip of rag
That fluttered like a flag,
As, with unwonted swirl, there blew a passing breeze.
But whence came human dress
Amidst that loneliness?
None cast away their garb amidst such wilds as these.

With lingering steps and slow,
To the great stone they go;
Oppressed with anxious thought,—for well their souls [divined
That, though the granite bore
All peaceful as of yore
Its front to face the light, dark mystery hid behind.

They looked: and there they viewed
A sight to chill the blood.
Stretched flat upon its back beside that great gray stone,
A woman's body lay,—
Part with'ring in decay,
Part wasted of its flesh down to the naked bone.

Her clothes about her spread
Torn rags. Upon her head
The jetty silken hair was deftly coiled and tied.
One small white tender hand
Was raised, as in command,
Pure from all taint or spot as if she ne'er had died.

But on that hand no ring.
Nor found they anything
That might her name, or rank, or aught of her declare ;
And naught of her is known :
Beside the great gray stone
She died. It thus befell about her coming there :—

Beyond the heights that rise
Above Glen Clova, lies
A neighbouring mountain glen, where Prosen's waters [roam ;
Far up the river stood
A worthy man's abode,—
A humble place, yet blest, a peaceful Scottish home.

One early April noon,
When sunshine brought its boon
To trick the hopeful hearts of those expecting Spring,
A woman stopped before
That quiet cottage door,
And craved to rest a while from weary wandering.

Noble her countenance,
Although the troubled glance
Of her dark eyes bespake a spirit much distraught;
Tall, stately, cold, and proud,
Her presence disallowed
The poorness of her dress, in plain town-fashion wrought.

Right welcome was she made.
Soon on the board was laid
The best of fare—milk, cakes, heath-honey sweetly strong.
She stayed but little space;
Then, with a haughty grace,
She rose, and said,—'Farewell. Steep is my path and long:

'It lies o'er yonder hill.'
Said the good-wife,—'It 's ill
At any time to cross, unless the road is known.
I wish that you would stay.
Pray do not go away
Till my good-man returns—you must not go alone.

'Oh! woman, do not go:
The clouds are full of snow'—
In vain she spoke to one who scorned to make reply;
The wanderer went forth
To brave the bitter North,
The majesty of doom resplendent in her eye.

Forth up the glen she went;
Her aim, or vague intent,
No mortal tongue hath told, and none will ever tell;
Perchance she went to seek—
Beyond the mountains bleak
And o'er the Isla's stream—some lost one loved too well.

Still onward does she keep.
She climbs Drumfolla's steep,
And panting gains the ridge; but as she left the lee,
Around her tempests broke,
While, like a cloud of smoke,
The mist came rolling up from chasmed Corrie Fee.

No thought has she to turn:
The fever-flames that burn
In her bewildered brain a maddening impulse send
Through all her frame. She speeds
Impetuous on, nor heeds
Or risk, or pain, or toil, so she but reach her end.

More thick the mist-clouds rise,
Obscuring earth and skies.
Alas! poor wanderer, most sorely dost thou lack
A strong and friendly hand,
To help thee to withstand
The fury of the blast, and keep thee to the track.

She struggles on and on.
The last faint light is gone:
Full in her tender face come blinding clouds of sleet:
Stunned, stupefied, and dazed,
Her whole perception mazed,
No more can she control the strayings of her feet;

And—ever making press
Against the tempest's stress,
Instinctively impelled by stubbornness of pride,—
She quits the narrow path,
And staggers straight for death,
Nearing the awful rocks that bound Craig Rennet's side.

Not yet her hour has tolled—
Some secret voice cries, Hold!
And guides her faltering steps along the Dounatt's height,
Above the great rock-rifts,
To where Craig Mawd uplifts
His scarped, tremendous form-- black as the shades of night.

Hark to that piercing shriek!
The eagle's ravening beak
Throws to the gale that cry: wild screams his answering mate.
Smitten with sudden fears,
The wanderer flees: she nears
Fiâlzioch's splash and glide o'er the smooth walls of slate.

Safely she passes; then
Descends unto the den
Where lawless men of old would oft in secret dwell:
There, plunging o'er the steep,
White-Water shapes his leap
Like to Death's courser's tail emergent from black Hell.

She feels her strength abate.
And now, to ease the weight
That clogs her tender limbs, their covering off she throws:
Then—by some mystic force
Impelled to keep her course,
And aided with new powers—barefooted on she goes.

On, on,—but not for far.
Ah! did some Heavenly star
Shine comfort, through the clouds, on that poor wanderer's [breast?
And through the furious storms,
Reveal bright angel-forms
Sent by the gracious Lord to bear her soul to rest?

Forward—a little space.
Her end comes on apace.
The frost-fang bites more keen, the fierce winds fiercer [blow.
She fails:—then, fainting thrown
Beside the great gray stone,
She yields herself to God amidst the ice and snow.

The eagle's distant yell
Pealed out her funeral knell—
A boding voice 'twixt earth and mist-enshrouded sky:
The ptarmigan's hoarse croak
Her parting requiem spoke:
The ghostly wild-cat screamed her last lone lullaby.

THE ROCKY MOUNTAINS.[7]

YE mountains of rock in the Land of the West,
Ye mountains of glory, for ever be blest!
Blest, blest be your valleys with vast craggy walls,
Your icy blue torrents and white waterfalls.
But oh! to be up on the heights, alone,
Where the pretty gray Siffleur sits still on a stone;
Sits on a stone and whistles and sings,
And trances the heart with his magic spell;
Sacredly sad his music rings,
Clear as the tones of a silver bell,—
Sounds that weep, that aspire, that pray,
Like angels calling a soul away.

How grandly, O mountains, your forests are spread
O'er the low sunny slope in the valley's deep bed,
How sweet the pine-fragrance that gladdens the air
In the haunts of the Moose and the grim Grisly Bear!
But oh! to be up on the heights, alone,
Where the curly-horned Mountain Ram dwells with
his own;

Dwells with his own on the pleasant steep,
Quenches his thirst at the glacier brook,
Crops the sweet grasses that crisply creep
To cover the sides of a sheltered nook;
Wanders a while, or rests at his ease
Basking in sunshine and screened from the breeze.

Magnificent mountains! when dawn has begun
How proudly your pinnacles shine in the sun!
Bright o'er your far summits gold fire-glories glow,
Then descend crag by crag to the valleys below.
And oh! to be up on the heights, alone,
Where the snowy Goat climbs on the chaos of stone;
Climbs the rock waste with his wide black feet,
Scales the ice-cliff whence the waters part,
Shades his thick fleece, from the noon-tide heat,
In the crater sunk to a mountain's heart—
Trees and green grass in the depths of it lie,
And a little blue lake that mirrors the sky.

Loved mountains! blest mountains! how fair, yet how strange,
When the moon overtops your majestical range!
Shows a thin radiant arc, straight leaps full into sight,
And illumes your vast caves with her silver-sheen light.

Then oh! to be down by the blazing logs,
In the midst of good hunters and horses and dogs.
Fragrantly smokes the resinous pine,
Tall is the spire of its broad red blaze,
The eyes of the horses like beryls shine,
The torrent glitters with golden rays.
Not a sound in the night but is near and small,
And vast is the silence that broods on all.

FEBRUARY IN THE PYRENEES.[8]

THE maidenly snow on the distant peak,
Pure child of the firmament, faultless born,
Gazed fair at the sun, who seemed to seek
To melt into mercy her virgin scorn.

And a stern black rock stood apart, and frowned,
For he envied the snow in her lustrous white;
And the grim gray shadows closed around,
In dread of the sun and his lordly light.

And the frail young beeches stood shivering near,
With their delicate branches brown and bare;
But a bird in the thicket sang loud and clear,
For he scented the Spring through the frozen air.

From afar on the wind came the shepherd's cry,
From the grassy slopes and the boxwood bowers,
As his mottled flock to their home drew nigh,
To rest at their ease in the long dark hours.

Then the sun went down, with a last caress
From his golden lips to the fair white snow,
And all Winter came with a deathly stress
On the heights above and the vales below.

Yet a loveliness walked in the quiet dale,
By evening's power from her thrall released;
For the silence spoke in a tender tale,
When songs and voices had sunk and ceased.

And silence itself more silent grew,
In the murmurous hush of the streamlet's tide
And the lull of the breezes, whispering through
The tall, sad firs on the mountain side.

EARLY MORNING.

THE morning is fair on the meadows,
Bespangled with lights from the dew,
And long are the misty gray shadows
Of holly and yew;
For low is the place of the beautiful sun,
Though darkness is ended and day has begun.

The blackbirds are merrily singing
In bush and in bowery tree,
The cow-bells are tinkling and ringing
O'er meadow and lea;
For every sweet cow is astir in the dell,
And moves to the music that moves from her bell.

And there are the calves with their mothers,
A gentle and innocent sight,
Some playfully dance with the others,
Some drink, with delight,
From the bountiful udders that pleasantly stream
And whiten their muzzles with rivers of cream.

Then away! through the broom and the heather,
To the heart of the forest of pine,
Where alders and birches together
Their foliage combine,
And shadow the pools that lie quiet and cold
Beside the lone graves of the warriors of old.

To the prickly gorse thickets are stealing
The ravenous creatures of prey,
The fox and the polecat, concealing
Their deeds from the day,
And the hedgehog is hasting, securely to sleep
Till the sun has gone down to the depths of the deep.

How sweet is the breath of the birches!
How mildly and lovingly grieves
The voice of the pigeon that perches
Among the green leaves;
And through the long grasses the fawn and the doe,
Like dreams in the wilderness, silently go.

Now the sun walketh up in his splendour,
And straightway all nature is fair;
With forces creative and tender
He comforts the air.
How rich is the glory, how thrilling the light!
There is life in the wild-wood when morning is bright.

IN SOUTH ENGLAND.

IT is beautiful day on the level moor,
 On the purple heathery sea,
There is never a voice in the breezes pure
 But the hum of the garden bee.

On a sandy hillock that fronts the day
 A white little cot is seen,
And it shelters its homely walls of clay
 In the bower of a fir-wood green.

And roses run wide on the cottage wall
 Through the tendrilled ivy's twine,
And the kindly clusters over them fall
 Of a newly-ripened vine.

In the shade of the porch there sits and sews
 A maiden of gentle bloom,
With a tint like the blush of the sensitive rose
 That is breathing sweet perfume.

She is tenderly soft as the offspring blest
  Of creatures small and fair,
And her figure is round as a ring-dove's breast,
  And like silvery-gold her hair.

With the nimble force of her shapely hand
  The needle bright she plies;
But she listlessly taps with her foot on the sand,
  And downcast are her eyes.

Ah, they gleam! she is fixing them now on the track,
  'Twixt the banks where green snakes play;
For her delicate ears have heard the crack
  Of a whip, not far away.

See, here is the team—the horses four,
  With their chests so broad and strong;
On their dappled coats the sunbeams pour
  As they drag the wain along.

It is cowslip yellow, that waggon brave,
  And its wheels are cherry red,
And it carries its tilt in an arching wave,
  Like a ship with canvas spread.

And beside the waggon there walks a lad
  Of the true old English stock,
With a buff straw hat, and his body clad
  In an olive-braided smock.

He is ruddy of face and fair and stout,
  And his arms are wide apart,
For two score of inches he measures about
  At the place that holds his heart.

All the gray-wing geese are down at the brook,
  And the spotted pigs go by,
And the hens scrape holes in the sandy nook
  Where the hives are ranged on high:

The beautiful maiden looks on from above,
  And her work aside is laid.
'Tis a winner indeed that shall win the love
  Of that sweet young Saxon maid.

THE GERMAN TOWER KEEPER.[9]

GOD bless our good prince, and establish his crown!
For I am the highest of men in his town.
Of women, however exalted in life,
The highest of all are my daughter and wife.
Yes, far above folks' heads we dwell,
And watch the town from hour to hour:
Their goings-on we see right well
From off the Margarethen Tower.

Our eight-sided mansion has windows all round—
We fear not foul vapours that cling to the ground,—
Whatever the weather, we get our full share
Of the warmth of the sun and the cool of the air.
No blinds shut out the light of day,
But every window has its flower,
And thus we keep a garden gay
Up in the Margarethen Tower.

Just under our feet are the tops of the limes,
Great trees of the ancient majestical times;
They spread their wide billows of blossom abroad,
And smell like a newly-made Eden of God.
Small birds and pigeons sing and coo
Within that fragrant yellowy bower,
And rear their young ones in our view
Beside the Margarethen Tower.

Hemmed in by the trees are the church's old tiles,
Which gladden our eyes with their ruddy-brown smiles;
High music the organ and choristers raise,
And encompass our home with an ether of praise.
We trust in God, and fear no shock
When lightning-clouds around us lour,
Nor when the furious tempests rock
The crumbling Margarethen Tower.

How pleasant to stand in the evening's soft light,
And watch the bright backs of the swallows in flight!
These angel-winged swifts heavenly messengers seem,
Though black be their plumage and piercing their scream.
Give, give me nature's blessèd tones!
Art's sweets compared with them are sour.
May swallows ever love the stones
Of our dear Margarethen Tower!

Three mighty great bells in the belfry are hung—
An earthquake for us when on holidays rung—
The big one a giant beneath it might hold,
The new one is less, but more precious than gold.
Cast from French cannon is that bell.
To Him who made the foeman cower
Its glorious notes thanksgivings tell,
From the brave Margarethen Tower.

And still, as the minutes creep stealthily on,
We notice the time when each quarter is gone,
And then little Süschen a crank works about,
And a block strikes the bell, and the thunder booms out.
Strange that a tiny tender maid
O'er sounds so great should have the power!
But weight by wit is always swayed,
As in the Margarethen Tower.

Well pleased are my wife and my daughter and I
To live by ourselves up aloft in the sky.
Our chiefest of wishes is never to part:
We are poor of the pocket, but rich of the heart.
Six old, four young, canary birds
Make little Süschen's only dower.
Oh, sweet is she beyond all words—
Joy of the Margarethen Tower.

God bless our good prince! As I sit here installed
And gaze on the spread of the Thüringer Wald,
Its heights all arrayed in the evening's gold glow,
I myself feel a prince o'er the city below.
God guard our prince and people well,
And every blessing on them shower—
On them, and me and mine that dwell
In the old Margarethen Tower!

IDLE TALK.[10]

MOTHER.

WIDE in the wild wood
Why wilt thou roam?
Safe with thy sisters
Stay thee at home.

DAUGHTER.

Murmur not, mother,
Maidens must play;
Working is weary,
Walking is gay.

MOTHER.

Home work is holy,
Hard thing but sweet;
Fiends ever follow
Far-straying feet.

DAUGHTER.

Ah! the good angels
Also are near,—
Go with me, guiding,
Guarding from fear.

MOTHER.

Thorn in the thicket
Tears with a cling,
Wasp in the woodland
Wounds with a sting.

DAUGHTER.

Richly red rose blooms,
Rarely smells he!
Happily hummeth
Honey-sweet bee.

MOTHER.

Banewort is baleful,
Blight-worm is dread;
Rough croaks the raven
Rending the dead.

DAUGHTER.

Kind coos the cushat
'Come to me;' so,
Lilting and laughing,
Lightsome I go.

A WILD-WOOD SPELL.

COME to the woods, Medora,
Come to the woods with me;
The leaves are green, the summer sheen
Is on the linden tree.

Up in the woods, Medora,
The thrushes warble free;
Around, above, they sing of love,
So let me sing to thee!

On the low thorn, Medora,
The finch is fair to see,
A jewel bright, a heart's delight—
Ah! so art thou to me.

From the dark pines, Medora,
There flows a balmy sea,
The air's soft kiss is heavenly bliss—
How sweet art thou to me!

Through the wood-moss, Medora,
The emerald lizards flee,
Away, away,—they will not stay,
Oh, flee not thus from me!

Come to the woods, Medora,
Come to the shade with me:
The roses bloom in that sweet gloom—
So bloom, dear rose, for me!

BONNIE BIRD.

ROAMING through the yellow wild
Before the trees were bare,
I met a pretty little child
With wavy yellow hair.

The sunset shed a yellow hue
And gilt the autumn gold,
And filled the pool with yellow too,
As full as it could hold.

Says I—'My bonnie little maid,
You are most heavenly fair!
From what sweet country have you strayed
To walk in yellow air?'

Says she—'I 'm only passing through
To lands of summer gold;
As all the pretty birdies do
That cannot bear the cold.'

THE MOUNTAIN FIR.[11]

THEY sat beneath the mountain fir,
Beneath the evening sun;
With all his soul he looked at her—
And so was love begun.

The titmice blue in fluttering flocks
Caressed the fir-tree spray;
And far below, through rifted rocks,
The river went its way.

As stars in heavenly waters swim
Her eyes of azure shone;
With all her soul she looked at him—
And so was love led on.

The squirrel sported on the bough
And chuckled in his play;
Above the distant mountain's brow
A golden glory lay.

The fir-tree breathed its balsam balm,
With heather scents united,
The happy skies were hushed in calm—
And so the troth was plighted.

FORGET ME NOT.

WHEN skies are blue above thee,
O maiden blue of eye,
Remember that I love thee—
A record is on high :
Forget me not, forget me not,
My token is the sky.

When little blue birds playing
Make merry in the tree,
Remember they are saying
A faithful word for me :
Forget me not, forget me not,
My token they shall be.

When blue-bells faintly quiver
As beams a gentle star,
Remember they deliver
A message from afar :
Forget me not, forget me not,
My token flowers they are.

When rivers blue are flowing
Where grass is green and new,
Remember they are showing
A promise in their hue:
Forget me not, forget me not,
My token is the blue.

THE WANDERING BEE.

A rare red rose on a terrace grew,
And rich was her odour and warm her hue;
A fair white rose to a ruin bent,
Tender in beauty and soft in scent.
Ha ha! ha ha! said the wandering bee,
Which of the roses has honey for me?

The rich red rose stands out in her place
And smiles to the sun with a broad brave face;
The strong bold breeze comes frolicking there,—
Lavish her welcome to sun and to air.
Ha ha! ha ha! said the wandering bee,
You are the friend in fine weather for me.

The sweet white rose clings close to the wall,
Where lovingly eventide sunbeams fall,
No rash rude storm can ruffle her breast,
Cradled in calmness and perfect rest.
Ha ha! ha ha! said the wandering bee,
You are the friend in rough weather for me.

AURELIA.

IN the glance of her eyes I marked a sheen
Of the sapphire blue and the emerald green,
And the red of the ruby rushed to streak
The lustreless pearl of her pallid cheek.
And she bent down her neck with a graceful power,
Like a swan that grasps at a floating flower;
And the waves of her bosom rose and fell,
Like the ample heave of the ocean swell.
Then she lifted her brow in majestic pride—
All doubtfulness vanquished, all cavil defied—
And, with accents more sweet than the boon from the bee,
She opened her lips,—and thus spoke she:—
'O thou whom I love! by what spell divine
Hast thou conquered my soul, and made it thine?
It is thine to thrill—it is thine to still—
Not a thought mine own, not a wish, not a will.

As the sun quits the morn in its beautiful might,
And escapes from the noon, but obeys the night,
So I—I have mocked at young love's young praise,
And I yield unto thee in the wane of thy days.'

Then I feel as a soul who, from pains and shame,
Is raised to a heaven in a car of flame;
For my arms in their circle all paradise hold,—
Though my locks are of silver, and hers are of gold.

BEAUTIFUL BASILA.

BEAUTIFUL Basila! thunder-browed maiden,
Eyed as a summer-gloom hurricane laden,
Regal as Hera, great queen of the sky;
Stately in stature, majestic of bearing,
Noble of spirit, nought dreading, all daring,
Proud as Athena, war-goddess most high!

Beautiful Basila! offerings thou owest:
Haste to the altars, and see thou bestowest
Gifts, like a mariner saved from the sea;
Much for thy comeliness, Heaven high adoring,
More for thy stateliness praises outpouring,—
Love-winning grace had been fatal to thee.

Beautiful Basila! hadst thou such sweetness,
All men would madden to win thy completeness,
Mocking at all other women that are:
Straight these thy body to fragments uprending,
Heav'n thy bright soul would for time never-ending
Set in the azure to shine as a star.

Beautiful Basila! guard thyself surely,
Trenched in thy haughtiness dwell thou securely,
Risk not a flight to star-regions above.
Yet if such life should e'er seem to thee lonely,
Change thou thy ways,—but to one mortal only,—
Change thou to me, for I long for thy love.

SELÊNÊ.

MY heart is lifted up on high
At thought of thee—at thought of thee.
All other maids, I pass them by;
They 've nought of thee—they 've nought of thee!

Oh, thou art like the mystic moon,
So gently glad—so gently glad.
Oh, thou art like a tender tune,
So mildly sad—so mildly sad.

The love within thine eye's gray deep,
All Heaven is there—all Heaven is there;
And gleams of Eden fondly sleep
Within thy hair—within thy hair.

Thy soul upon my soul outflows
So full and free—so full and free,
That all, in most divine repose,
Is filled with thee—is filled with thee.

BETTER THAN GOOD.

IT is better than good when the heart is light
To wander alone where the wild woods spread;
Where the fir-tree boles are mossy and white
And their dragon limbs are smooth and red,
And the grave-green canopy overhead
Houses the scent of the resinous balm—
Sweet, pleasant tears that the pines have shed,—
And from quiet heather and branches calm
The birds and the bees uplift their psalm.

It is better than good when the heart is drear
To wander alone by the ocean's side;
Where clamorous sea-mews sailing near
Make mournful music to meet the tide,
Which rolls to the rocks with a witless glide,
And roars, and batters the steadfast stone,
And broken falls as the boulders guide;
While in creek and cavern the waters moan,
And the dungeoned tempests howl and groan.

But whether the heart be merry or grave,
It is best of all that is held as good—
Though the blasts and billows of ocean rave,
Though the birds and the balms be sweet in the wood
To walk with a woman of gentle mood,
Whose soul and body are chaste and fine
And bright in the splendours of maidenhood,
And to know that her body and soul are thine,
For life on the earth and for life divine.

GOLDEN PIGEONS.[12]

I.

GOLDEN pigeons! lightly flitting
Through the silver morning sky;
Fire-enkindled forms! emitting
Meteor-gleams of mystery;
Is it kindly, is it fitting,
Thus to show yourselves on high?
As I view you, twisting, turning,
In your magic might of dress,
All my soul is parched with yearning;
Your unearthly loveliness
Scorches all my soul with burning,
Pain from pleasure's pure excess.
'Rash upbraider! blame the Sun.
His the glow, ourselves have none.'

II.

Saintly woman! restful sitting,
Tender children round thy knee;
Queenly-humble,—sweet submitting,
Calm out-breathing majesty;

Is it kindly, is it fitting,
Thus to show thyself to me?
As I view thine all-perfection,
Far I seem to stand apart;
Much I doubt mine own election,
Raised to empire o'er thy heart;
Filled with grief, I dread rejection
From that heav'n wherein thou art.
'Dear upbraider! thus I shine
In love's own light—it is not mine.'

HEART'S-EASE.

HEART'S-EASE! ah, dearest one, methinks
That I alone can fitly tell
The might of blessedness that links
And twines itself—as in a dell
The woodbine circles withered trees,
And rainbow-garnishes their gray—
Around a weary, wayworn heart,
Which soon must bid a long farewell
To youth and all its joyaunce gay,—
Through one fair thought, from all apart,
Richer than golden stores of Art,
Sweeter than Pleasure's honey-cell:
This, that for thee and me beyond death's seas
Two lives will join for aye, two hearts find ease.

HIDDEN NOT STOLEN.

DEAREST, Death could have no terror
Either for myself or you,
Save for this our simple error,
That his coming parts us two.
Whether you or I be taken,
Wherefore should the other sigh ?
One—blindfolded, not forsaken ;
One—unseen, but not less nigh.
True-loving souls each other close enfold,
For aye, 'mid earthly gray or heavenly gold.

Like the bud that blooms to petal,
Blossom souls in heaven above :
But, as magnet draws the metal,
Love will draw its fellow-love ;
Even so when sense is shrouded,
Tombed in trance or slumber's night,
Soul draws soul in realms unclouded,
Loving there in limpid light.
Our faithful souls no destiny shall sever,
For fast they cling, at last to join for ever.

FIRS AND FOXGLOVES.[13]

O BLOOMING bed of foxgloves
  Fair on the island set,
Incarnate lovely essence
Of air and rivulet!

O hoary host of fir-trees,
Embodied warmth of years!
I call on you to witness
My sorrow and my tears.

Ye smiled on all our meetings,
Ye wept to see us part:
O things of strength and beauty,
Replenish ye my heart!

NOVEMBER SNOW.

THE snow upon the rose-flow'r sits,
And whitens all the spray ;
Sweet Robin Redbreast o'er it flits,
And shakes the snow away.

The snow upon my life-bloom sits,
And sheds a dreary blight :
Thy spirit o'er my spirit flits,
And crimson comes for white.

IN RICHMOND PARK.

WHY stands she there so solemn
Beside the whispering water,
Like some memorial column?
What misery hath sought her?

Why all so black and lonely
In yon wide meadow stopping?
The deer around her only,
The fragrant herbage cropping.

Her vesture, crape-enshrouded,
Would seem the outward token
Of sorrows closely crowded
Beside a heart half-broken;—

And mark the kerchief's whiteness
Across the sable going,
To meet the minished brightness
Of eyes with anguish flowing!

Full many a one, lamenting,
Will compass mournful pleasure
Where Nature unrelenting
Bestows her sternest measure, –

Amidst the rhythmic thunders
Of ocean's endless story,
Or 'neath the weirdly wonders
Of forests old and hoary;

Or where from gulfs abhorrent
The mountain rears its steepness,
Or where the furious torrent
Descends to darksome deepness.

And likewise there are mourners
Who love to lie and languish
In quiet nooks and corners,
To calm their spirit's anguish,—

'Mong gracious garden roses
Behind the yew-tree screening,
Or where the brake discloses
Wild blossoming and greening;

Or where the river stilly
Moves gently in its gliding
Through reed and water-lily,
And loathes to leave its hiding.

Thus some, with Nature's madness
And frenzy of turmoilings,
Would crush their sullen sadness
In vast pythonic coilings.

Thus some, to Nature's mildness
Their weary spirits bringing,
Would charm away the wildness
Of sorrow's cruel stinging.

But thou, poor lonely woman!
What find'st thou in that station—
Displayed to gazers human—
Of comfort's revelation?

No might dwells there to awe thee,
Grim sorrow's force out-stressing;
Nor peaceful power to draw thee
From tyrant grief's oppressing.

Yea! stand'st thou there as martyr?
In mystical emotion
That scorns for joy to barter
One drop of poisoned potion?

And therefore in the meadow
Forlornly stand'st thou dreaming,
A black mysterious shadow
In the pale sunset's gleaming?

Yet, may be, self-compassion
Within thy soul hath spoken,
Declaring through what fashion
Thy bonds might best be broken;

And in the peopled loneness
Of this vast park of pleasure
Thou find'st a subtle proneness
To yield thy heart a treasure.

As the dun deer go straying
Around thy silent figure,
Perchance in thee are playing
Some spells of joyous vigour,

Empowered to lift thy musing
Beyond the woeful present,
Its sombreness transfusing
With memories fair and pleasant.

For God's kind forest-creatures—
Great Nature in them dwelleth;
They form her smiling features,
Whence all her love out-welleth:

And, like to children tender
That know not guile nor sinning,
Their spirits slim and slender
Breathe effluence sweetly winning.

Say, dost thou feel that essence,
Thou solitary weeper?
And brings it back the presence
Of a loved infant sleeper—

Thine infant fondly cherished?
And doth the influx cheer thee,
No more to deem it perished,
But feel it moving near thee?

Or dost thou feel, caressing
Thy widow-woeful fancies,
A touch of perfect blessing,—
At which thy spirit dances?

A touch as softly falling
As thistle-down alighted,
Strong thought of him recalling
To whom thy love was plighted—

The sharer of the sweetness
Of all thy earthly being,—
Who fled with angel fleetness,
And vanished from thy seeing;—

A soul of nurture simple,
Who loved the life that quivers
Beneath the airs that dimple
The forest lakes and rivers;

Who loved the dell deep-holden
Within the greenwood mazes,
More than the mansions golden
Where fashion blares and blazes;

And counted wild-wood haunters—
The deer of spirit tender—
Far lovelier than the flaunters
In palaces of splendour.

So, dost thou seek thy vanished
Where he most oft hath found thee,—
Where man is seen but banished,
And wild things roam around thee?

O poor unfriended mourner!
My spirit flies to greet thee:
Ah! think me not a scorner,
But let my spirit meet thee;

Yea, meet thy spirit, bringing
Such balm to heal thy sorrow,
As prayers and sighs up-winging
From angel stores can borrow.

THREE SCENES.

WITHIN THE HOUSE.

The new-made widow waits and muses.

THEY tell me that my love is dead:
His flower of life, so sweetly blown,
On the unthankful desert strown,
Its beauty crushed, its fragrance shed.

Within this room where shadows sleep,
Alone I lie and strive to mourn;
But something laughs my woe to scorn,
And cramps my heart,—I cannot weep.

My love is dead, they tell me so:
Yet still before my soul he stands—
A traveller held in distant lands,
Not gone for evermore—ah no!

Ah, say not that the lands are far
Where my belovêd one doth roam:
He hath but wandered from his home,
To walk where woods and mountains are;

To look upon the lights that burn
In golden glory o'er the hill,
To listen to the murmurous rill;—
Soon, soon, my darling will return.

I see him! garnished with the grace
That freely through the forest flows,
With airs of honey-bloom and rose,
With Eden glowing in his face.

His eyes with ecstasy are fraught,—
As a mild wood-dove feeds her young,
They nurture mine with gladness sprung
From loveliness by Nature wrought,—

And splendour circles round his head;
He speaks like breezes that entwine
Their softness with a stately pine—
He lives strong life—he is not dead!

Not dead—yet why this weight unknown
That holds my heart in voiceless woe,
This pressure of a tyrant foe?
O power that fetters! let me moan.

BEHIND THE HOUSE.

A Savoyard Girl, with a marmot and a hurdy-gurdy, plays, sings, and dances.

Far away from my mountains,
From the waft of the breeze;
Far away from my valley,
From the flowers and the trees;

Far away from my mother,
In a dull distant land,
I must sing and make music
With the turn of my hand.
Merry bird in the pear-tree, that warbles and sings,
Take my heart to the mountains, far away, on your wings!

Dear, pretty, little marmot,
Do you long to be free?
Or are you more happy
To be nestling with me?

Sweet and kind are your eyes, dear,
And you 're soft and you 're gray;

You are good, and you love me
In the land far away.
Merry bird in the pear-tree, that warbles and sings,
Take my heart to the mountains, far away, on your wings!

BEFORE THE HOUSE.

The Funeral moves on.

They bear him along on their trusty arms—
And the pall is wet with an April shower—
Adown the valley and past the farms,
To the clang of the bell in the ivy tower.

They bear him along to the graveyard gloom,
And they leave him a while to rest in the day;
For the folk must sing, and the organ boom,
And the mournful vicar must read and pray.

But soon they raise him, and off again
With a slow, uncertain, solemn tread;
And there follows him close a sable train,
The men that are nighest of kin to the dead:

And they set him down at the grave betimes,
Where by weeping maidens a hymn is sung;
While, high overhead, from the tops of the limes,
Come the cry of the rooks and the plaint of their young.

Then the vicar prays the prayers that are meet,
And the coffin is laid in the clammy ground:
Yet the early flowers are both gay and sweet,
And the vicar's dog goes wandering round.

And away go the folk, with a saddened mien,
With steps that halt and with tongues that pause:
But they see the old limes in the sunlight sheen,
And they list to the rooks with their callous caws;

And strong nature's might in their veins they feel,
And their life-blood thrills as they briskly walk;
So half-glad, half-sorry, their hearts they steel,
And smile grows laughter, and whisper talk.

Lo, this is the way of the world to-day;
It will yet be the way of the world to-morrow:
And he who would sorrow, and he who would pray,
Should pray all alone, and alone should sorrow.

LEAVES AND WATERS.

WHEN faded leaves are falling
On idle waters—crawling
Heart-weary of their way,
To where the rivers rushing
In force of flooded flushing
Move with majestic sway—
I listen to the weeping
Of the stilly rain-drops, steeping
The forest in decay.

They whisper,—O thou being!
So sorrowfully seeing
The gay green forest's fate,
Thy life is but a seeming,
The shadow of a dreaming,
The symbol of a state:
Like to the leafage wasting,
Slow crawling on, or hasting,
To black Oblivion's gate.

I answer them,—O daughters
Of sunshine and of waters!
Man is not like the leaves,

Which glad the forest growing,
Then fading fall,—and flowing,
  Away from Earth that grieves,
Adown the rushing river,
Go vanishing for ever
  To where the ocean heaves.

His being doth resemble
The water-wastes that tremble
  To meet the sun-god's ray,
And rise to him; then falling
At weary Earth's recalling
  Deject a while they stay;
Till breathes their bridegroom burning,
And straight to him returning
  Once more they rise to day.

Ah, rain-drop! man is brother
To thee, and ne'er another
  Of Nature's soulless birth;—
No creature formed to grovel
In planetary hovel,
  Fast fettered to the Earth;
But framed to follow dancing
The love-beams that are glancing
  From Eden lands of mirth.

ILLUSION.

OH, what contentment lies
In grace of summer skies
That warm the wintry world and make it fair to scan?
No might have they to still
The ever-flowing rill
Of restless vague desire that haunts the heart of man.

The billowy bloom that sleeps
Among the woodland deeps
Displays its priceless store to tempt our yearning sight;
Yet when we fain would hold
Queen Nature's lavished gold,
And coffer it to serve for coming days' delight,—

Ah then, with mocking dip
The treasure-glories slip
Perfidious from our clasp, and vanish into space:
And there we sigh and moan,
More sorrowful and lone
Than had we ne'er beheld those witcheries of grace.

E'en thus, what meets the ear
When forest-murmurs cheer
The sick despondent soul with lullabies of song—
The cooing resonance
Of mingled tones, that dance
So solemn and so sweet, so tender and so strong,—

It makes but mockery
Of him who fain would try
To garner in his heart that rapture of a dream:
It fades, it fades in mist,
And he is left to list
The sullen-throated roar of Life's old turbid stream.

STRENGTH AND BEAUTY.[14]

A HUNDRED fathoms, each doubly told,
Soars the rock-rampart, dark and cold,
Above the rush of the silvery river;
Its awful caverns gape like graves,
Oft through its crags the tempest raves,
The thunders roar, the lightnings quiver.

The eagle deems it a home too bleak,
And sails away with scornful shriek
To mock the storm-cloud's threatening mutters.
On the topmost peak of the cliff I lie:
Death reigns—alone with him am I—
Lo! over yon rift, a butterfly
Flits up and down with weak white flutters.

EARTH'S BEST.

'TWAS an evening warm and still:
Wandering went I o'er a hill
Fragrant with the fir-tree balm;
Airs celestial round me moving
Breathed the bliss of heavenly loving,
And steeped my soul in sacred calm.

Perched on summit of a pine
Sang a Robin, purely fine;
Mournful-mellow music came
Trilling from his tiny beak,
Flutes and viols seemed to speak
Within his throat of ruddy flame.

Proud he perched upon the tree,
Poised on yellowy fir-buds three
Lifted o'er their parent green;
Timed to every swelling note
Sank and rose his ruddy throat,
And nought but sweet was heard or seen.

Ah, methought, if all my days
Wandered on in woodland ways,
Sights so fair to glad mine eye,
Sounds so sweet mine ear to greet,
Scents so rare with all to meet,—
No! never could I bear to die.

THE MOORLAND MOTH.[15]

WHENCE dost thou stray,
Sweet creature soft and golden;
Why cease thy stay
Among the oak-trees olden,
Sacred, and gray?
Work'st thou some lovely duty,
With magic of thy beauty?

Thou more than soft!
Thou ravishingly mellow!
What Seraph doffed
His tunic—tender yellow
As skies aloft
When evening sunbeams clamber
Arrayed in woven amber,—

Doffed it to spread
All o'er thy head of wonder,
Then loving led
The robe around and under,—
Golden as bed
Where the sweet wood-bee dallies
Within the lily's chalice?

O'er thy slight wings
Dark shade he gathers meetly,
Lest envious things
Discover thee too featly;
But pearl he brings,
And stars them each with whiteness
To garnish them with brightness.

Child of the skies!
From thy sweet form outvoicing,
Clear whispers rise
That call me to rejoicing:
As bells call some
To merriment and wedding,
While many tears are shedding.

It speaks not words,
But in my soul I read them;

As songs of birds,
Though there be none to heed them,
Kiss the gold chords
Of Nature's noble lyre
And make the music higher.

So the moth tells
Of sympathy supernal,
That springs and swells
In radiancy eternal
From heavenly wells,
Perennial in the duty
To fashion endless beauty.

LOST MUSIC.

IN morning times of infant cheer,
When everything is heavenly clear,
The heart is not for loving meet :
Its chords are all too frail a toy
To utter choruses of joy
For mid-day's unbeshadowed heat.
Too lightly strung, too frail a toy, to utter choruses of joy.

In noontide days of manhood's might,
When everything is sunny bright,
The heart is all for loving strong :
Its chords are far too fondly fain
To utter the melodious strain
Of mid-day's ecstasy of song.
Too nimbly strung, too fondly fain, to utter the melodious strain.

In evening days of olden drear,
When everything is sad and sear,
The heart is not for loving trim :
Its chords are far too feebly bound
To utter the sonorous sound
Of mid-day's mellow-measured hymn.
Too weakly strung, too feebly bound, to utter the sonorous sound.

FAREWELL.

WOULD that I were young again!
Roaming through the forest glen,
Where the solemn fir-trees sigh,
Rivers running golden by.
My youth—my youth—will none restore?
No more—no never, never more!

Lovely dreams—and idle dreams
Up the rocks and o'er the streams,
Where the birches balmy smell,
Heather-bloom, and foxglove-bell.
My youth—my youth—will none restore?
No more—no never, never more.

Weary moan—and idle moan!
Calling joys for ever flown.
'Mong the quiet garden flowers
Happy halt mine evening hours:
Till youth—my youth—the Heavens restore
Once more—for ever, ever more!

COULEN FOREST.[16]

MUSE of the North, who lov'st the land of Ross,
From Cromartie to distant Applecross,
Draw near, and help an all too daring swain,
Who sings the glories of that fair domain
Whose ancient woods and spreading waters stay
Beneath the shield of towering Ben Eây.

Amidst the pines a gabled cottage stands,
Where Coulen's stream its narrowed course expands,
Whose sheltering porches, walls of brilliant sheen,
Bespeak the light and love that dwell within.

* * * * * *

When radiant morn illumes the purple moors,
Rise, favoured inmate, happiness is yours!
By sleep's soft mystic spell your force increased,
Go share the bounties of the morning feast:
Then forth,—and find, awaiting your behest,
That sport or pleasure you may love the best.

If, by good fortune, it should prove thy joy
To wile the salmon and his kindred coy,
Bring forth thy rod, bid long adieux to care,
And launch thy coble upon deep Loch Clair;
Or cast thy fly across the rippling wave
That smiles and dances round the Giant's grave.
Or, yet intent to swell thy basket's store,
Traverse the bounds of heathery Monimore,
And claim the finny treasures that lie hid
Within the depths of dark Loch Eălid;
Removed from rule and precedent thy fate,
Should evening find thy heart disconsolate.

Dost thou belong to those who love to throw
The leaden shower against the feathered foe?
Pursue the grouse that throng these mountains fair,
Surprise the ptarmigan in Corrie Lair;
E'en as thou lik'st it,—toil, or seek thine ease,
At least thou livest in the fragrant breeze;
Meet is thy pastime—better things away—
To fill the moments of an idle day:
Take my good-will; I find no warmer words
To sing thy triumphs over vanquished birds.

Hail! brethren true, who love the nobler way,
Who harm not birds but make the stag your prey;

Come, guile the monarch in his well-watched hold,
Drive the swift bullet through his heart of gold.

* * * * * *

Well shot! True course the rushing cone has made:
He shrinks: he stops: he droops his stately head.
Slow move his faltering limbs: in vain he tries
To evade his doom; he sinks, no more to rise.
Oh joy! Behold his antlers' ample round:
Crowned are their summits—yea, and doubly crowned.
No shepherd's staff their mighty span could cross,
Rough as the rock, black as the inky moss;
Brow, bay, and tray, each point complete appears—
A range of bayonets,—nay, a plump of spears!
Ah! what a strong delight my being fills:
Pale grow the memories of a thousand ills:
Let griefs and losses, sickness, cares, combine
To sap my life—this hour at least is mine!

Ah, let not my rough rapturous strain perplex
The tenderer fancies of the gentler sex;
Nor cause them think no joys may here be sought
Save those familiar to the hunter's thought:
Pleasures supreme, enchanting, yet remain,—
Of angel sweetness, pure, without a stain.
Is there no joy to wander o'er the hills,
Roam through the woods, rest by the rippling rills;

Bask in the heather where the sunbeam shines,
While breezes sing melodious through the pines;
Or hand in hand with happy children roam,
And hear sweet talk of love, and peace, and home?

How pleasant too 'mid dreamy hours to float
On Clair's still bosom in the tranquil boat,
And mark the glorious scenes upreared to view:
The embattled steeps of craggy Scoür-dhu;
Or him, the Titan old, vast Ben Eây—
Stony his face, his aspect stern and gray,
Yet down his visage silvery torrents glide,
Like tears of anguish, sorrow conquering pride:
Or, dark as storm-clouds ere the crash comes on,
Black Liugach, watching rock-bound Torridon.

1871.

THESEUS: A BALLAD.

NOW who is this that journeyeth along the cavern lone?
The light of day comes faint and gray, and hidden waters moan.
Grim is the place and wan and wild, no pleasantness it hath,
Great rugged rocks and boulder-stones are scattered on the path;
And oft this wayfarer must press through crannies dank with slime,
And oft-times o'er a rocky wall he painfully must climb.
Fair armour doth his form embrace, majestical of mould;
And naked bears he in his hand a sword that glints like gold;
And still he windeth out a clue, as virgin silver bright,
Whose thread shall be a guiding line to bring him back to light.
Whence came that golden-gleaming sword to Theseus (whom ye see),
Thus bravely metalled for the hands of heroes great as he?

'Twas Ariadne's loving gift,—the daughter she, I ween,
Of Minos, kin to gods above, and of his crownêd queen;
And Ariadne, clear of wit, the clue to Theseus gave,
To lead him from the mazy den which else had been his grave:
For nigh the labyrinthine track through rocks asunder riven,
A monster foul and fierce abode, accurst of earth and heaven.
On youths and maidens was he fed, whom there they would entomb;
He smote them with his cruel horns, and rent them in the gloom.
Now Theseus, offspring of a king, had sailed the salt seas o'er,
To end that thing of monstrous brood, the loathly Minotaur:
So here behold him on his way along the fateful path,
Where light of day comes faint and gray, and life is lapped in death.
An hour he travelled heedfully, but nothing did he meet,
Though many a rusty skeleton he trod beneath his feet,
Till the long cavern opened wide, and day began to spring;
Then Theseus, at the further end, beheld a grewsome thing:

The brutish likeness of a man, on giant limbs upreared:
But huge above the brawny chest a bestial head
appeared,—
The head as of a mighty bull, with nostrils broad and bare;
The human body, vast and wan, was bristled brown with
hair.
Red fire was rushing from its eyes, it stamped the cavern
floor,
It uttered sighs and mournful moans, stark mad for
human gore.
But Theseus, casting down the coil, his sword before
him shakes,
As one that stirs himself anew: then with a roar that
wakes
The rock foundations from their rest, the thunderous
brute comes forth,
Like to the winds of winter wild on waters of the
North.
But 'twixt the keen and polished horns, which shed a
fitful glow,
And o'er the knotted coils of mane, Prince Theseus struck
his blow,
Fair on the hidden fount of life that dwells within the
spine:
And down the loathly monster dropped, as drops a
mountain pine,

And bellowed forth his utmost breath with one convulsive thrill.
Thus died the accursêd Minotaur—and all the cave was still.
Said Theseus, as he wiped his sword upon that monster's side,
'When to the lordly Attic land I come across the tide,
And, great in name and high in fame, regain my kingly hall,—
Lo, I will hang this head on high to deck the marble wall.'
Then turned the hero on his path and backward went his way,
The labyrinthine cavern through, to lightsome realms of day:
To realms of joyful lightsomeness, for Ariadne fair,
As mild as Aphroditê's dove, is waiting for him there;
And swiftly through the cloven rock, where hurrying torrents flow
To meet the briny water-flood, together forth they go
Adown unto the ocean shores, and there a bark they gain,
And speed for Attica the blest, across the emerald main.

ANDROMEDA: A BALLAD.

ALL on the shores at Iopa a mournful maiden wept;
The wandering billows on the sea ran laughingly and leapt;
The ripples of her sunny hair were smiling to the skies,
Wan was her face with wild despair, and fountains were her eyes;
Like silver in the golden day her beauteous body shone,
Dark fetters hung around her limbs; and there she stood alone.
Then suddenly the waters swelled, and from the ocean caves
There issued forth a mighty snake, that towered above the waves.
He opened wide the ghastly gap his crested head below,
Where fangs like bare bones in a grave were champing to and fro,
And set his grim and greedy eyes upon the maiden near;
Against the purple cliff she lay, entranced with utter fear.

Close came the serpent, from his jaws he scattered clots of foam,
He bended back his crest to strike,—when, from the azure dome
A ray of magic, flashing bright, threw lustre on his face,
And one who rode on golden wings descended on the place.
A buckler in his hand he shook, and lo! there was revealed
A visage wreathed about with snakes, full on that warrior's shield.
Then, quickly as the furious flame that rages far and near
Will shrink aghast unto the earth, and hiss with sudden fear,
When over it the torrent flows, invincible of might,—
So, hissing dropped the snake, his blood congealing at the sight
Of sad Medusa's visage drear, with tireless eyes that mock;
And straight this serpent did become a rigid form of rock.
Then to the maiden Perseus went (the warrior thus was hight),
And scarcely set on her his eyes, for pity of her plight,
But drew in manner of a veil her hair across her breast,
And drew it round her body bare, which swoonêd lay at rest.

Thereafter from the maiden's limbs the brazen chains he
tore;
And gave her to her watching kin, who led her from the
shore
And brought her to her royal home. Then Perseus
straightway came,
And from King Cepheus, as was meet, his guerdon he
did claim.
So Cepheus and Cassiopê, her sire and mother, there
To Perseus gave, to be his wife, Andromeda the fair.

DEA INCOGNITA.[17]

FAIREST and sweetest! the love-light is playing
Soft on thy tresses, like melodies straying
O'er the long ripple of southerly waves;
Womanhood's essence within thee is dwelling,
Marvels and mysteries songfully telling
Forth from the deeps of the mystical caves.

How from the soul of thee fragrance is rushing!
Springs of delightsomeness swelling and gushing,
Flooding my heart with unspeakable grace,
Æther of joyfulness out from thee wending;
All of my nature, in unison bending,
Bows to the might of thy beautiful face!

Whence is the glory-flood over me streaming?
Glow of trance-vision, remembrance of dreaming,
Light from the shores of the slumberous sea—
Silent in solitudes dimly reposing
Far from the glamours of outward disclosing—
Home of the spirit of all things that be.

Lo, in the womanly curves of thy forming,
All that is bountiful, all that is warming,
  Mingles, and mazes and maddens the sight;
Order's eidôlon the oval expresses
Clothed in the sheen of thine exquisite tresses—
  Motherhood's ovoid of archetype light.[17]

Warm in thine eye-glance Creation is wooing,
Casting a spell with a whisper of cooing;
  Majesty passive is framed on thy brow;
Delicate cheek of symmetrical moulding,
Rose-bringing honey-mouth pureness enfolding,
  Witness Love primal incarnated now.

Thine the quintessence of finest and fairest,
Thine the most typical richest and rarest;
  Thou are the Eden thyself, and the Eve.
Nature's own goddess-hood in thee thou bearest,
Livest in, joyest in, over thee wearest,—
  Formed for a gladness, yet fated to grieve!

Man cannot woo thee and make thee his treasure;
Time cannot move to Eternity's measure,
  Thou art a symphony sung from the sky:
Hopeless I yearn for the primal perfection
Imaged by thee in illusive reflexion;
  If I forget thee not, hapless I die.

Sweetest! all-beautiful! list to my wailing;
Cast on thy loveliness gauzes of veiling,
  Lay the white veil on thy locks of dim gold,
Cover thy glory of gladness and sadness,—
Ere my wrought spirit escape into madness,
  Leaving my body to melt in the mould.

THE SORROWFUL VARANGIAN.[18]

BRING me the oak-leaf and the blue-bell bloom,
To deck Melissa's earth-encompassed tomb;
To blend in beauty with the reeds that wave
Their feeble arms around her forest grave.

Bring me a cordial for my soul's despair;
Draughts of strong life, to shatter into air
These deadening sorrows on my senses laid,
That hold me helpless as a mournful maid.

Bring me rich wine to play the kindler's part,
Fill me with force and renovate my heart:
Tears have no might to prove a sorrow's truth;
Haste ye! restore the vigour of my youth.

Bring me the spear, the battle-axe, the blade,
'Stead of this mattock and poor peaceful spade!
Soon, O Melissa, round thy grave shall go
The cowering shades of them that wrought thee woe.

O loveliest woman! lovelier than the rays
From yonder lord of heaven that broadly blaze,
Moon-like thou glidest on the shadowy shore,
And I, forlorn, shall see thy face no more.

VENDETTA.

'O LOVELY little mountaineer,
Now wherefore do you hide,
With musquetoon and bandoleer,
And dagger at your side?'

She smiled from eyes of torrid glow,
And oped her boddice' breast;
Between the blooming hills below
A lock of hair was prest.

'I cut it, steeped in rueful red,
From off my murdered brother's head.
There, singing, comes the slayer: wait,
And see me lay him stark and straight.'

THE PINE MARTEN.[19]

I WALKED in Glen Tanar, when glory was falling
At dawn of the day on the stately old trees,
The river sighed low, and the roe-deer were calling,
The pines of the forest sang songs to the breeze.
Around the red branches a marten twined,
His soft fur glowed and his bright eyes shined;
Glowing and shining,
Twisting and twining,
A dove and a serpent combined.

O Cynthia! false Cynthia! such graces adorning
Thy soft supple form, yet untrue to thy vow!
I have lived on thy promise to meet me this morning:
Just like to that treacherous marten art thou?
Around my heart thy wiles have twined,
And into my soul thine eyes have shined;
Glowing and shining,
Twisting and twining,
Thou dove and thou serpent combined.

Ah no ! here she comes, through the heather-bells moving,
Beside the tall foxglove that bends o'er the stream.
Thou angel all-bright ! dost thou deign to be loving ?
Ah ! surely this joy is no more than a dream.
    Around my heart thine arms are twined,
    And into my soul thy soul hath shined ;
    Glowing and shining,
    Twisting and twining,
    Soft dove and sweet serpent combined.

THE EAGLE.[20]

O'ER the rocks of Glen Clova in dark Corrie Fee,
An eagle was soaring, triumphant and free;
The bright water was leaping from crag unto crag,
And the echoes rang loud with the roar of the stag.
Higher, bird, higher go,
Broad wings of fire throw,
Higher and higher
Soar like the fire,
Up o'er the hills and away!

In a black city garden, confined in a cage,
An Eagle is pining, in sorrow and rage;
The rough wheels make their rumble, the smoke-vapours fly,
And the mob throngs unceasing—the Eagle will die.
Lower, poor Eagle, go,
Lone in thy regal woe,
Lower and lower,
Far from man's power,
Off to the shades and away!

To the rocks of Glen Clova come, maiden, with me,
The sweet grasses are waving, the flowers call for thee ;
Leave, oh leave the dull cities, their crowds, and their care,
Come away to the mountains and breathe the wild air.
Higher and higher go,
Love-flames like fire glow,
Higher and higher
Glow like a fire,
Up in the hills far away.

DISENCHANTMENT.

IN dreams I love thee wildly,
When soul to soul flies free,
And mystically mildly
My being twines with thee.

Ah how, from dreams returning,
Thine influence haunts me still!
My soul is sick with yearning,
Mine eyes the tear-drops fill.

We meet on earth: but vainly
I look for magic there,
Thy words come poorly, plainly,
Thy face it is not fair.

THE HALO.

DEAREST, that halo round the moon,
Which charmed us in its rainbow light,
Seemed a true type of love; but soon
It passed, and all was shimmering white.

Then, dearest, came a thunderous cloud,
And o'er the moon's pale disc it rolled,
As 'twere sweet nature's mournful shroud;
And all was dark, and all was cold.

Ah! dearest—dear to *me* for aye,—
Our love was once as rainbow bright;
Soon its warm colour passed away,
And then came clouds—and all is night.

FAIR FELLOWSHIP.

AH! if in loving me
Worlds of delight there be,
Heed not the vengeance that lurks to destroy.
Care can but pleasure quell;
Forth let thy being well,
Gladden my spirit with rivers of joy!

Ah! if in loving me
Danger and wrong there be,
Mine be the anguish, the grief, and the shame.
Woman must suffer woe:
Glad to reproach I go;
Strong in thy manhood proceed thou to fame.

'Ah! if in loving thee
Sorrow and shame there be,
Full must we share them in sharing delight.
Sun being sunk in shade,
Gloom on the earth is laid:
Day be our portion, or nethermost night!'

HEART'S-NEED.

THE mountain maid is singing free,
The mountain shepherd whistles high:
There 's joy for her—why none for me?
He loves to live—and why not I?

The mountain maid has homely fare,
In lowly dress her limbs are clad:
I dainties share, and silken wear,—
But she has got her shepherd lad.

The shepherd braves the stormy breeze,
The winter snow, the sultry sun:
In golden rooms I rest at ease,—
But he has love, and I have none.

In vain, in vain my anxious mind
Seeks joy on earth or calm above:
One only thing I needs must find—
A heart to meet mine own with love.

NEVER AGAIN.

FOR ever, for ever, for ever and a day,
For ever, ever lonely—my true love gone away;
For ever, for ever,—the words are light to say,
But oh! to feel the sorrow, for aye, for aye, for aye!

No, never,—no, never,—no, never, never more.
No, never hear his kind voice as in the days of yore;
No, never see his noble face, and love him and adore.
But oh! my heart, what anguish is gnawing at the core!

For ever, for ever, for ever be thou blest!
No, never,—no, never, come trouble to thy breast;
For ever, for ever, abide thou in thy rest.
But oh! I mourn to lose thee, my dearest, sweetest, best!

POOR LOT'S WIFE.

IN all the days, the many days, since ever I was young,
I never met a Highlandman with such a pleasant tongue.
So pleasant, so pleasant, so debonair and free:
Oh yes, oh yes,—you 'd never guess the things he said to me.

Oh those were days—were days indeed! and all the world was dear;
For then the bonnie Highlandman spoke music in my ear.
So pretty, so witty, so debonair was he—
O dear, O dear, it came to pass he spoke of love to me.

Alas, alas,—the days!—the days! his arm around my waist—
The hours! the hours!—he 's dead and gone, a bullet through his breast.
So gallant, so gallant, so debonair—ah me!
But yet, but yet, one must not fret, the thing was fixed to be.

The nights and days! the weary days! I only wished to
die :
But time brought comfort in a while—and *you* came by
and bye,
So ruthful, so truthful, so amiable to me—
Oh yes—oh yes—I ought to bless the day I met with thee.

STAG'S-HORN MOSS.

THREE maidens played on the green, green ground,
And with Stag's-horn moss they wreathed them round:
Hands on high and hands across,
They twined a merry maze with the Stag's-horn moss.

And what, oh what, is the fate they twine
For the maid that is sweet as the eglantine—
Jessamine cheeks and golden hair?
Oh, she shall live in love and have gold to spare.

And what, oh what, is the fate they tell
For the maid that is bright as the heather-bell—
Rosebud cheeks and hazel hair?
Oh, she shall live in love and have children fair.

But what is the fate the long moss weaves
For the maid that has locks like the autumn leaves—
Lily cheeks and auburn hair?
Oh, she shall die in love when the woods are bare.

FOND HOPE.

THERE are blooms on the mountain and flowers on
  the lea,
And love is in bloom in my bosom for thee:
But love it is fanciful, love it is free
As breeze of the forest, or billows of sea.
  Lovely little Leila, be loving to me!
  Never was a maiden so lovely to see.
  Lovely little Leila, my life is in thee!

There are ripples and sheen on the beautiful lake,
And scents of the heather and birch are awake:
But cold on the precipice water-waves break,
And jeer at the granite, and quiver and shake.
  Lovely little Leila, be patient with me!
  Never was a maiden so lovely to see.
  Lovely little Leila, my life is in thee!

Thine eyes they are azure, the hair of thy head
Is touched with the tints of a leaf that is dead:
But wild on the firmament vapours are spread,
And glory is vanished and happiness fled.
  Lovely little Leila, be faithful to me!
  Never was a maiden so lovely to see.
  Lovely little Leila, my life is in thee!

LOST HOPE.

THE fires of love are dead and cold,
The tale of blessedness is told,
The songs of mirth and joy are o'er;
My Leila lies beneath the mould,
On earth to wake no more—no more.
Lovely was our merry dream,
Gladsome as a summer gleam:
But oh, it was an evil dream
to leave one sorrowing sore!

I will not weep and make my moan:
A pleasant artifice is known
To wounded hearts that ache at core;
They use the pangs that are not shown,
To burst their life,—and forth they soar.
Come, ah! come thou hither, Death!
Welcome is thy wintry breath:
For oh, a goodly friend is Death,
to open such a door!

MAIDEN OF THE MERRY-MAKING.

MAIDEN of the merry-making,
Leave, leave me lone!
Say, why such trouble taking,
Smiling to a stone?

Eyes—were they gray and dreamy,
Not black as sloes;
Cheeks—were they lily-creamy,
Rather than moss-rose;

Locks—were they soft, not curling;
Lips—far less red;
I might think thee like my darling—
Ah me! my darling dead.

LILY LORN.

LAMENTING and weeping she went through the wood
To the vale where the home of her father had stood :
The place was a wilderness, silent and lone,
The cottage a ruin, the garden o'ergrown.

All rank grew the nettle and rough in its mien,
As it marred the gray wall with its coarseness of green ;
And high grew the foxglove, cold comfort to tell,
As it dangled each dainty and delicate bell.

She laid herself down in the depths of the grass,
And her soul from her body was longing to pass ;
So mourned she and wept she, so wild was her woe,
That her spirit seemed fain with her weeping to flow.

'O father! O mother!' in anguish she sighed,
'How sweet was the home where we loved to abide.
Gone, gone! ah, alas for your sorrow and need,
When ye sank, broken-hearted,—and mine was the deed!

'Ah, why did I wander so far from my own,
From the hearts that were proved, from the love that
was known?
Oh! alas for the love that was nought but a lie:
It is dead—it is dead—and deserted I die.'

Then a whisper came softly as flowerets might fall,
And as kind as the cooing of doves when they call:
'Lament not, my Lily; no more will I roam,
I will be to thee father, and mother, and home.'

MOLLY THE MELLOW.

THE melon is mellow and dainty and rare,
  And mellow is Moll of the ashy-brown hair;
The peaches are soft and the apricots gay,
But softer is Molly and sweeter than they.
  Oh! softer than nectarine, sweeter than pear,
  Is Molly, my Moll with the ashy-brown hair.

There 's a rose that is gentle and tender and sleek,
And gentle is Moll of the creamy-white cheek;
The rose is as fair as the foam of the sea,
And sweet with the sweetness of blossoming tea.
  Oh! gentler than lily or jessamine meek
  Is Molly, my Moll of the creamy-white cheek.

The mavis sings sadly, the wood-pigeon sighs,
For love of my Moll with the olive-green eyes:
The mavis and linnet, the siskin and dove,
Are lovely and loving, but Molly is Love.
  Ah! sweeter than sweetness—ah! lovely alone—
  Is Molly the mellow—my Molly, my own!

THE FLITCH OF DUNMOW.[21]

COME Micky and Molly and dainty Dolly,
Come Betty and blithesome Bill;
Ye gossips and neighbours, away with your labours!
Come to the top of the hill.
For there are Jenny and jovial Joe;
Jolly and jolly, jolly they go,
Jogging over the hill.

By apple and berry, 'tis twelve months merry
Since Jenny and Joe were wed!
And never a bother or quarrelsome pother
To trouble the board or bed.
So Joe and Jenny are off to Dunmow:
Happy and happy, happy they go,
Young and rosy and red.

Oh, Jenny 's as pretty as doves in a ditty;
And Jenny, her eyes are black;
And Joey 's a fellow as merry and mellow
As ever shouldered a sack.

So quick, good people, and come to the show!
Merry and merry, merry they go,
  Bumping on Dobbin's back.

They 've prankt up old Dobbin with ribands
    and bobbin,
  And tethered his tail in a string:
The fat flitch of bacon is not to be taken
  By many that wear the ring!
Good luck, good luck, to Jenny and Joe!
Jolly and jolly, jolly they go.
  Hark! they merrily sing.

'O merry, merry, merry are we,
Happy as birds that sing in a tree!
All of the neighbours are merry to-day,
Merry are we and merry are they.
O merry are we! for love, you see,
Fetters a heart and sets it free.

'O happy, happy, happy is life
For Joe (that 's me) and Jenny my wife!
All of the neighbours are happy, and say—
"Never were folk so happy as they!"
O happy are we! for love, you see,
Fetters a heart and sets it free.

‘O jolly, jolly, jolly we go,
I and my Jenny, and she and her Joe.
All of the neighbours are jolly, and sing--
"She is a queen, and he is a king!"
O jolly are we! for love, you see,
Fetters a heart and sets it free.’

POOR OLD TOM.

IN the Spring-time of my days, when my life was new
begun,
My pleasures they were many, but little worth each one;
There was running, jumping, playing,
There was climbing, nesting, straying;
I had all that sort of childish fun.

In the Summer of my days, when my life was in its force,
My pleasures they were many, and gallant was their course;
There was gambling, poaching, roving,
There was drinking, fighting, loving;
I was strong as any farmer's horse.

In the Autumn of my days, when my life was running
through,
My sorrows they were many, my pleasures they were few;
There was wiving, childing, thinking,
There was striving, toiling, sinking;
I had little strength, and much to do.

In the Winter of my days, now that life is nearly gone,
My sorrows they are many, my pleasure is but one ;
There is shaking, coughing, wheezing,
There is aching, shivering, freezing ;
But it 's nice to sit and bask in the sun.

GOOD OLD SOULS.

MY dame is old, and I am old,
We 're dazed and dim, and dull and cold:
But what care I, and what cares she?
We 're happy folk whatever be.

Time was when she was young and gay,
Would smirk and smile, and dance away:
Though dancing does not now agree,
We jog on happy, I and she.

And I was once a lively boy,
Would sing my song, and pipe for joy:
No more of piping now for me,
Yet all our days are harmony.

We do not bill and coo and kiss;
A loving hug would come amiss
To old rheumatic bones, you see:
But that is nought to her and me.

In summer, when the sun is hot,
We toddle round our garden plot;
And bask a bit, and watch the bee:
It hums for joy, and so do we.

And when the winter snows and blows,
We sit beside the fire and doze;
Or laugh and chat and drink our tea,
With—'Here 's to you!'—from her and me.

Our earthly race is nearly run,
We 're getting both so old and done:
But bodies old as old may be
While souls are young, so what care we!

For when it 's time for us to die,
We don't intend to say Good-bye:
Since neither death nor life, you see,
Shall part my dear old dame and me!

PART II.

ROSELIP AND CHERRY.

BENEATH a fir-tree, planted
Hard by a rocky brow,
Sweet Roselip sat, and chanted
A ditty to her cow.

Her golden hair was flowing
All flossy o'er her knee,
Her eyes were violets blowing;
And twelve years old was she.

And thus she sang:—Dear Cherry,
I love you night and day,
You are so kind and merry,
So pretty and so gay.

I like to see you wading
Across the sunny pool,
To where the alders, shading,
Keep all the pasture cool.

I like to watch you chewing ;
I sit and never stir,
And listen to the cooing
Of pigeons in the fir.

Oh! how I love, my Cherry,
To stroke your velvet nose,
So dear to me—so very :
Your eyes are like the roe's,—

The roe whose children slender
Frisk round us in the glen ;
They know our hearts are tender,
Although they flee from men.

Yes, when you walk sedately
You are a queenly cow ;
Your head so grand and stately,
A crown upon your brow,—

A lovely shining crescent,
Just like the quiet moon
That makes the evening pleasant
Among the flowers in June.

Your sides are soft and yellow,
Like pretty cream and whey;
Your chest is white and mellow,
Your legs are silvery gray.

How sweet the gentle showers
Have made our birch-trees smell,
And all the purple flowers
Of heath and heather-bell!

The fresh young firs are giving
Their fragrance in the heat—
What pleasure to be living
Where everything 's so sweet!

See how the water glances
Above the fairy falls;
And down below it dances,
As people do at balls—

But this is much too silly!
For how can I or you,
My darling Cherry-lily,
Know what the people do?

Come, come, my pretty rover!
You must not roam at will
To crop the crimson clover
And blue-bells on the hill.

For now it 's hot and sunny
We 'll stay among the fern,
And watch the bees make honey
From flowers beside the burn.

I 'm selfish—yes, I see it
In her reproachful eyes:
I like the shade—so be it,—
She does not like the flies.

And when they tease her sadly
With stings and bites and buzz,
Away she scampers madly—
That 's what my Cherry does!

My pet! don't mind their teasing,
Their angry bites and stings;
The nights will soon be freezing,
And kill the cruel things.

Oh, winter-time is dreary!
It 's hard to live at all;
Yet you are snug, my dearie,
And happy in your stall.

Alas! the years go flying,
Just like a sad, sad tune:
And then we shall be dying—
But not, I hope, quite soon.

My darling! may we never,
Oh never, never part!
To lose thee, love, for ever,
Would fairly break my heart!

No further could the maiden
Beyond this fancy get;
With choking sobs o'erladen,
She hugged and kissed her pet.

THE ORPHAN BOY.

THE pretty little Orphan Boy –
He wanders on alone;
He cannot sing a song of joy,
And yet he cannot moan—
His heart is like a stone.

His father was a valiant man
Who fell in battle wild;
A lion when the fight began,
But gentle as a child--
So merciful and mild.

His mother was a woman sweet
As ever loved and wed;
Too pure for Earth and too complete,
Her soul to Heaven had fled—
For she was lately dead.

And no one loved the orphan now,
Or said a tender word,
Or kissed his fair and holy brow,—
Or came at night, unheard,
To soothe him if he stirred.

And no one came to laugh and play,
And smooth his silky hair;
And no one cared to hear him say
His simple infant prayer—
But the Good Lord could care.

God sent an angel from above,
The mother of the boy;
Invisible, she breathed her love,—
Vouchsafed the blest employ
To fill his heart with joy.

At first he smiled a happy smile,
Such comfort she supplied;
But sorrow touched him in a while,
And so he wept and sighed—
And laid him down and died.

Then variegated butterflies
Came flitting from their bowers,
And hovered o'er his opened eyes,
Supposing they were flowers
Made beautiful by showers.

The pretty little orphan's soul—
Because on Earth distrest
With grief that nothing could control—
Had gone to Heaven, to rest
Upon the mother's breast.

LOST IN THE FOREST.

OLD Winter was buried, and Spring with a song
Had brought in sweet Summer, the merry and strong;
And the wood-bees were humming where honey-bloom climbs,
And the fir mingled fragrance with flowers of the limes.

See, see, in the forest, where nature is fair,
A woman is wailing and rending her hair;
In all the green hollows, o'er all the wide wastes,
She lingers distracted or desolate hastes.

'My darling, my darling, my own little child,
Oh where hast thou wandered alone in the wild?
All the night I have sought thee--alas, for the morn!
Thou art dead, O my darling, or dying forlorn.'

Say why does she halt, with a pause and a start,
Like a doe when its body is pierced by a dart?
At the foot of an oak, by the boughs overspread,
She sees her sweet baby—and thinks he is dead.

For quiet he lies on the carpet of moss,
With one arm stiff and straight,—but the other across,
And its tiny white fingers with delicate tips
Are asleep on the swell of the rose-blossom lips.

She gazed in a trance, till her spirit had grown
As the icicle-drop in a snow-covered stone :
But a wren flitted past by the face of the child—
Then he opened his eyes, saw his mother, and smiled.

As fleets through dark cloud-land a sunbeam of joy,
So flew she to pour out her soul on her boy :
And the vigilant angels were smiling above,
And their crystalline spirits were lovely in love.

GOOD-BYE TO PHIL.

GOOD-NIGHT, my darling little Phil,
No longer must you stay;
For I am far too weak and ill
To talk to you and play—
Perhaps I 'm going away.

They tell me it 's a happy land,
Where all good people go;
And there your master soon shall stand,
And leave you here below:
Ah, Phil! I think you know—

You look at me so earnestly,
And droop your pretty tail,
And make your tiny whining cry,
As if your heart would fail—
Your face looks almost pale!

O Philly, how we used to run
  In our belovêd wood,
When all my lesson-work was done,
  As quickly as I could,
  And we were out for good.

Ah, wasn't it a lovely place,
  So pleasant and so still!
And through the heather we would race
  Around the sandy hill,
  And hunt the rabbits, Phil.

Or through the bramble and the fern
  We merrily would hie,
And hares from cunning corners turn,
  And make the pheasants fly
  With such a startled cry!

And oh, how nice it was to ride
  On Lily round the parks;
While you would follow at her side,
  Or chase the rising larks,
  With happy bounds and barks!

And in the early summer-time,
  When trees were smelling best,
High up the spruces I would climb
  And peep into each nest,—
  While you would pant and rest.

And sometimes, where our favourite brook
  Beside the garden flows,
For water-rats we used to look;
  And when the bubbles rose
  Before your dainty nose,

How loud your angry little shriek
  Would make the echoes ring,
As eagerly you 'd dance, and seek
  To catch the diving thing;
  While pebbles I would fling.

O Philly, had I strength again
  In this small weary arm,
I would not give poor creatures pain,
  Nor try to do them harm—
  My heart has grown so warm.

My father and my mother dear—
It 's sad to see their pain:
But death comes closer year by year,
And no one can remain—
We all shall meet again;

And walk, they say, in lands of light
Where angels come and go,
And shine more beautiful and bright
Than any words could show—
And must *you* stay below?

O Phil! my Phil! it can't be true
That never shall you see
The fair and happy countries too
Where I so soon shall be—
You 've been so dear to me!

Your loving spirit from afar
Will seek me when you die;
Beyond the highest, highest star
Your love will bear you high:
For love has wings to fly.

THE FIDDLE-CASE.

HARD by a mighty railway station
Whence bales and boxes went all day,
Two birds held friendly conversation,—
A sparrow and a starling they.

'Strange creatures men!' said Master Sparrow,
'See how yon youth with elfish locks
Puts his neat parcels in the barrow,
But lugs about a plain deal box.'

'Sir,' said the Starling, 'cease your wonder;
That box a curious thing contains,
Which makes a sort of squeaking thunder,
As when a love-sick cat complains.

'And this indeed I count a riddle,—
Why men should like such doleful groans?
Why they should crowd to hear the fiddle,
Yet pelt the love-lorn cat with stones?'

'Well,' said the Sparrow, 'tastes must vary,
Let none the judge's seat usurp;
Some like the shrieks of the canary,
I like my mate's melodious chirp.

'But birds like us of birth and station
May stoop to learn e'en from an ox:
Much food there is for contemplation
In this same fiddle and its box.

'The outside merely deal discloses,
A common thing that none esteems;
But lo! within, a beast reposes,
Most powerful in howls and screams.'

A poet heard: 'My brain were narrow
Could I not wisdom win,' said he,
'From such a very sapient sparrow,
An Aristotle on a tree.

'Henceforth when I, 'mid fashion's bustle,
Change smiles for smiles and knocks for knocks,
I'll tell the apes that round me hustle—
"This is not me, it is my box."'

RHYME AND REASON.[2]

SAID Mr. A. to Mr. B. :—
'Why is it we so often see
Among the poets now-a-days—
From him whose forehead wears the bays,
Down to the vilest poetaster
Whose rightful wreath were sticking-plaister,
To heal the marks of foul disaster
Encountered by his erring crown
When outraged critics knock him down—
Why is it that the most sublime,
As well as those who cannot climb
Out of the ditch of idiot slime,
Display so little love for rhyme,
And breed the mermaid thing one knows,
Half fishy verse, half female prose?'

Said Mr. B. to Mr. A. :—
'I really can't pretend to say
What are the bogies more abstruse
That scare our poets from the use
Of that which is the sauce and juice
Of heavy verse-joint: any goose,

However dull and short of sight,
May see the common fiends that fright
A stripling scribbler, who aspires
To vent the big poetic fires
That scorch his inwards, yet desires
That this same fiery gas should spout
Without much pain in coming out.'

Said Mr. A. to Mr. B. :—
'I 'm *not* a goose—and I can't see.'

Said Mr. B. to Mr. A. :—
'You *are* a goose—a goosey gray;
If see you can't, then listen, pray.
The common fiends that vex and spite
A fellow who in rhyme would write,
Are headed by a pair of brothers:
Good rhymes, the elder hides and smothers;
The younger brings the evil others.'

Said Mr. A. to Mr. B. :—
'Although so very rude to me,
And bitter as the busy bee
That stings your nose to show his glee,—
For sake of knowledge (priceless bliss!)
I 'll pardon all you 've said amiss,
If only you will tell me this—

Tell me the truth with visage sad,
Extenuate nought, and nothing add :—
What are good rhymes? and what are bad?'

Said Mr. B. to Mr. A. :—
'Repentance wipeth sin away.
I pardon thee—once more be gay!
Wit's sun shall shine, so make thou hay.'

'The perfect rhyme is true in chime,
Is true in spelling, true in time,
The LOVE and DOVE is perfect rhyme.

'The next is perfect to the ear,
Though to the eye a little queer;
The DEAR and BEER let no one jeer.

'The third is perfect to the eye,
Though to the ear a little shy—
The GOOD and FOOD a man may try.

'The fourth, imperfect both in chime
And spelling, keeps a perfect time.
To use it some account a crime,
But Pope, and all the old sublime,
Delighted in the DEATH-FAITH rhyme:
Do likewise, ye who high would climb!

'Nor dread such rhymes as BEE or SEA,
Paired off with words like HARMONY—
A most melodious sort of rhyme,
Though out in spelling, chime, and time.'

Said Mr. A. to Mr. B.:—
'If all those matters disagree
Yet nothing 's wrong, it seems to me
That nothing *can* be wrong—d' ye see?'

Said Mr. B. to Mr. A.:—
'Sweet friend! thy doubts I 'd fain allay.
With Pope and Dryden one may stray,
Yet all the while securely stay
Within the light of English day.
But with the modern pedagogue,
You 're apt to wander into fog,
And stick in some outlandish bog.

'The DEATH and FAITH 's imperfect rhyme,
The Y-BEE-SEA 's imperfect time,
Relieve a weary faultless chime,
Like stone-work mixed with bricks and lime.'

Said Mr. A. to Mr. B.:—
'Your kindness sounds a jubilee

In my young soul. On bended knee
I prithee, friend, impart to me,
What sort of rhymes to none are free?'

Said Mr. B. to Mr. A.:—
'The hunt is up! away, away!
The hounds give tongue, the bugles bray—
Off lumbers our unsavoury prey—
Let 's kill him, then his brethren slay!

'—Nay, spare poor FOUL and FOWL the small,
'Tis but a simple cuckoo-call,
'Tis scarce an *English* rhyme at all.
Nor heed his sister LIME-SUBLIME,
A careless echo, not a rhyme.
But ha, "Iago! blood, blood, blood"!
Here 's one most fit for wormy food—
Death to the JACKDAW-BACKDOOR brood!
Likewise that imp of kindred spawning,
The loathly reptile MORNING-DAWNING.'

* * * * *

Here comes a break, for Mr. B.
Unluckily had failed to see
That rhymes so infamously queer
Brought torture to the tender ear
Of one who happened to be near.

It was the old retriever, Nero,
That chanced to be this hapless hearer ;
A dog as gallant as a lion,
With sides of steel and limbs of iron,
Yet, like the ancient tune-slain cow ill,
He now gave such a doleful howl
As might have touched a Stoic's bowel.
And as the Cockney poison bored
Within his frame, he writhed and pawed ;
Then fled his spirit to the star
That glads remote America—
Or twinkles in the dim boudoir.

Said Mr. A. to Mr. B. :—'Ah,
I feel quite ill—O dear! O deâr!'

Said Mr. B. to Mr. A. :—'As
You feel I feel—alas! alas!'

With rabbit-power the venom bred,
And through the air contagion spread.
Cries Mr. A., 'I'm dead—I'm dead!'
And soon his sweet young life was sped.
Stout B. no more could stand the poison,
He felt that he must also die soon ;
Wolves would have wept had they but seen him

So tortured in the duodenum
By diabolical venenum.

Hi! hi!—some friends come by—Hi! hi!
They hear his faint despairing cry,
And fain would they some succour bring
With water from a neighbouring spring.
But ah! he lay in pain uncommon,
In anguish to be cured by no man;
Nor even by the fairest woman
That ever exercised her free-will
In doing good or doing evil!
His sand was run, his sun was set.
No leech from holy Haymarkêt,
In haste to earn an honest penny,
Fond of a case and fond of a guinea,
Could find a physic strong enough
To cure what he was dying of.
No cordial of which man was 'ware
Could make him competent to bear
Such foul effluvium in the air—
Not even that bright spring-watêr!

And soon, alas! he cannot swallow,
In vain they slacken his shirt-collar;
Low lies the beautiful Apollo.

His bloom is shed as faded rose's,
His visage pallid as the snow's is,
His heart is chilly as his toes is!

He turned upon his back and diêd,
And went to rest in endless quiet—
And presently the rest expired!

THE ELM AND THE ROBIN.

A Robin perched upon a bough
Puffed out his ruddy breast;
Says he, 'Of every tree, I vow,
I love this Elm the best.

'How high she rears herself in air,
How grand her summer green,
How proud in winter, stript and bare:
My noble forest queen!'

The merry woodman whirls his axe,
The Elm-tree bows her head,
Her last strong buttress yields and cracks—
She falls, for ever dead.

The Robin nimbly flutters down,
Unmournful at her fate,
And peers through all her shattered crown
For flies to feast his mate.

LITTLE SWALLOWS.

LITTLE swallows four are peeping
Plump and patient from their nest,
Placidly their vigil keeping,
Tawny-throated, fair of breast.

Now the mother-bird is bringing
Store of baby-swallows' food :
Yonder see her! fleetly winging
Homeward to her hungry brood.

This time one, the next another,
From her kindly beak is fed ;
Chiding not the favoured brother,
Each awaits his daily bread.

Soon from the small nest departing
Gladly seek they Nature's gifts,
Through the endless æther darting
With the martins and the swifts ;

Over houses, under bridges,
Round the fields where cattle graze,
Following gnats and flimsy midges
In the pleasant summer days.

But when frosts of autumn glitter,
All the swallows, in a row,
Sit and sing and chirp and twitter,
Telling tales of sun and snow.

Thus a while their plans they ponder,
Ere begins their wondrous flight;
Then across the seas they wander
Far away to lands of light.

ROBIN IN THE WOOD.

BIRD of red bosom and delicate beak,
Come with thy murmurous music, and speak
Songs to my spirit that yearneth to thee!
Gladden my heart with thy comely completeness,
Thou fair little image of niceness and neatness,
Thou essence of berry and blossom and tree.

Soon as I enter the sunny green wood
Swiftly thou meetest me, merrily rude;
Surely thou lovest me, soft little thing?
Feeling the tenderness forth from me welling,
That witches thee near with a friendly compelling,
E'en as a magnet the metal will bring.

Why, what a toy thou art, ruddy and round,
Hopping so high like a ball on the bound—
Jerky and perky, and utterly sweet!
Gazing about with such airs of astuteness,
While simpleness heavenly and worldly acuteness
Seem in thy starry-bright glances to meet.

Good is thy fellowship, brave little bird!
Deep in the wood, where no voices are heard
Breathing of man and his measureless woe.
Ah! what a love in the cushat's complaining,
That floats on the breeze, with a fragrance remaining
Reft from the blooms that in solitude blow.

Ha! Master Squirrel! what com'st thou to see,
Chiding and chuckling at Robin and me?
Why such a passion of anger and fright?
Harm shall not come to thee, poor little fellow!
Safe is thy skin so enchantingly mellow,
Goldenly ruddy and creamily white.

Up the high spruce-tree! abandon thy fears,
Lower those sensitive tufty brown ears,
And curl up thy brush with a confident air!
See, the bold Robin is fearlessly tripping
Full in the reach of my axe, that is chipping
Bark from the trees which I mean not to spare.

Robin, sweet Robin! I doubt that, at best,
Selfishness dwells in thy beautiful breast,
Leads thee so close to my footsteps to move;
Snatching the insects I start from their mazes,
When marking the timber with death-bearing blazes—
It is not on me that thou lookest in love.

Never mind, Robin boy! life is too brief
For testing the worth of a kindly belief:
Trustfully look at me, tenderly sing;
So shall I count thee a friend and a lover,
And nothing but heav'nliness in thee discover—
Thou sweet little, dear little, round little thing!

FRANKIE.[23]

A Little Irish boy was Frank,
Who near the Liffey stayed,
And daily by the river's bank
He carried on his trade.

A humble trade—but humbleness
Unwealthy people suits—
A vulgar trade, no more nor less
Than blacking shoes and boots.

Poor little Frank was twelve years old,
A puny boy and pale;
His brushes he could hardly hold,
So weak was he and frail.

He laboured morning, noon, and night,
And custom quickly came,
The folk took pity on his plight,
For he was likewise lame:

So lame he scarce could crawl about,—
Some fellow, whisky-'glorious,'
Had kicked poor Frankie's hip-bone out,
'O'er ills of life victorious.'

But wondrous are the powers that stay
In those who can't adjust
Their habits to the mirthful *may*,
But to the mournful *must!*

Nay more, content and pleasure lurk
In labour deftly done:
Young Frankie learned to love the work
By which his bread was won.

And putting, though no cultured boy,
His heart into his duty,
He found a meek artistic joy
In bringing boots to beauty.

So sweet his suffering-seraph face,
And tender, patient eyes,
And gentle, melancholy grace,
That people, in surprise,

Would stand and gaze with pitying stare,
  And murmur at the fate
That doomed a child so softly fair
  To pine in low estate.

And many an honest, worthy man,
  Whose heart with love was gushing,
His boots would straight begin to scan
  And vow they wanted brushing.

Thus penny payments, boot by boot,
  From morn till day's decline,
Made Frankie's purse of stocking-foot
  A perfect copper-mine.

Then, heavy task for one so frail,
  He 'd slowly lift his pack
And travel homewards, like a snail
  With goods upon its back..

For Frankie, I would have you know,
  Was furnished with a home,—
No vagrant hustled to and fro,
  For ever bound to roam.

Yes, Frankie had a happier lot
  Than many a lordly dweller
In palaces where love is not,
  For in his lowly cellar

A loving mother waited him,
  And little sisters five,
Whom he, although so frail of limb,
  Could help to keep alive.

And ne'er in mansions of pretence
  Were cheerier scenes, mayhap,
Than Frankie pouring all his pence
  Into his mother's lap.

Then kindly would she kiss her boy,
  So noble, brave, and true;
The little sisters, full of joy,
  Would come and kiss him too.

Soon round the steaming supper-pot
  They 'd make such loving mirth,
The room would seem a sacred spot,
  A humble heaven on earth.

Outside was one who 'd gaze and gaze
With envy in his face,
And wish that he might spend his days
In that most pleasant place.

'Twas Jim,—a great unlucky lad,
A silent, sullen fellow;
No sort of training had he had
To make his nature mellow.

A homeless stroller of the town,
In daily want of food,
The lad would wander up and down
And labour where he could.

Oft would he work among the coals
In some old collier-barge:
They 'd flog his jacket into holes,
Then give him his discharge.

He 'd fetch or carry, dig or hew,
Drive swine, or gather sticks;
Alas! his halfpence still were few,
While many were his kicks!

A savage, sulky lad was Jim,
  A hog all tusk and bristle,
A nettle in the stinging trim,
  An Ishmael of a thistle.

Rough weed! for thee there wept no showers,
  No sunshine on thee smiled:
But God delights in all His flowers,
  Both garden-plants and wild.

And Jim, on earth, was taught to swell
  Heaven's grand hosanna cry;
For glorious on the outcast fell
  The dayspring from on high.

* * * *

Return we now to Frank a while,—
  At work beside the river,
Rejoicing o'er his penny pile
  And thankful to each giver.

Behold a scurvy, scoundrel lot,
  Who watch the child by stealth,
And plan a miserable plot
  To rob him of his wealth.

'Tis sunset. See, with weary strain
  Poor Frankie homeward limps:
He nears a dark and dismal lane—
  Out rush the savage imps!

As when the patient Osprey toils
  To capture fish for food,
And bears away her glittering spoils
  To glad her hungry brood,

Down swoops the bald Sea-eagle—whish!
  And, ere his talons touch,
The cowering Osprey drops the fish
  She carries in her clutch,

So trembling little Frankie yields
  What he can keep no longer:
But ah! submission seldom shields
  Weak boyhood from the stronger!

These fiends (or, may-be, embryo saints)
  Are not content to rob,
But beat poor Frankie till he faints,
  To finish up the job.

And oft again they worked their will,
Delighted with the prank
That made the little cripple's till
Their steady savings-bank.

But things will sometimes go amiss
With villains and extorters,—
Down comes an angry Nemesis
From unexpected quarters.

And Ishmael Jimmy—who but he!—
Shall be the stout redresser,
To set the poor oppressed one free
And chasten the aggressor.

Too often Fortune fails to bring
(We farmer-folk can tell it)
The very man who wants a thing
To him who wants to sell it;

But now, as gentle as a dove,
A kindly part she played,
And brought the lad who wanted love
To him who wanted aid.

As Jimmy once in hungry vein
Watched Frankie at his supper,
The lower instincts of his brain
Severely jogged the upper;

And, through the vigour of the shock,
A spark of mental light
Enkindled somewhere in the block
A notion clear and bright.

Accordingly, as Frankie sat
Next morning on the Quay,
Came Jimmy to him (lads like that
Are introduction-free),

And there and then did Jim propose
A treaty of alliance,
Through which young Frank might set his foes
Completely at defiance.

Terms fixed:—*Imprimis*, Jim shall smite
The thieves of Frankie's hoard;
Secundo, Frank shall every night
Give Jimmy bed and board.

And, mind you, 'twas no paltry pay,
  For Jimmy's nightly lodging
Was just where he contrived to stay
  By means of skilful dodging:

And sometimes he would rest behind
  The pillars of a Club;
Or, like Diogenes, would find
  Much comfort in a tub;

Or, greatest of all joys, would draw
  Close to some bakehouse flue,
When the grim Myrmidon of law
  Had stalked away from view.

Once Jim and other lads of note,
  Birds of a kindred feather,
Beneath a bottom-upwards boat
  Kept *open* house together.

A happy summer house, but soon
  Cold winter nipped their fun:
Though ventilation is a boon
  It may be overdone.

Come frost, come storm, come misty blights,
They merely closer crept,
And through the long, long winter nights
They shivered as they slept.

At length, descending in the dark,
A mighty fall of snow
Entombed the poor old crazy bark
With all the lads below.

There, like to sparrows in a trap
On which the brickbat falls,
They struggled hard to find a gap
Or pierce their prison walls.

And, kneeling, with their backs they strove
To lift the weighty block :
Alas ! the boat no more would move
Than limpet from a rock.

Then Jim and his companions seven
Set up a doleful shout :
Policemen, passing (sent by Heaven)
O'erheard, and dug them out.

'All 's well that ends well '—but for some
  Misfortune knows no ending,
And Jim was ready to succumb,
  When luck, for once befriending,

So kindly whispered the *ideal*,
  To which his deep devotion
Would likewise help him in the *real*—
  A noble Foreign notion.

* * * *

Now, reader, back again to Frank!
  The sun had made its round;
Our boy had left the river's bank,
  His steps were homeward bound;

And flickering on his face there shone
  The dreary, doubtful smile
Of one who valiantly goes on,
  But trembles all the while.

And soon that dreadful place he nears,
  That dark secluded lane,
Where hide the enemy: his ears
  And eyes are on the strain.

Oh terrible! though help, he knew,
 Would certain come as fate,
Thinks Frank—'What ever shall I do
 If Jim arrives *too late!*'

Hark! screeches, whistles, curses clang—
 A peal to please the Devil:
Out rush the ragamuffin gang
 And lay poor Frankie level.

But suddenly their fiendish fun
 Was strangely brought to check,
And such confusion was begun
 As when upon the deck

Of pirate ship a bomb-shell grounds
 And sends the fragments flying:
'Tis Jimmy, who with tiger-bounds
 Arrives where Frank is lying,

And unexpected grace extends,
 Expressed in bounteous blows,
To these who thought themselves his friends
 But find themselves his foes.

N

And like as with a top that spins,
As faster fall the lashes
The more capacity it wins
For furious darts and dashes,—

Thus Jimmy—every trick they try,
He merely strikes the stronger.
He smote the sinners hip and thigh,
Till fight they could no longer.

Then with some valedictory shoves
He put the business through:
And sweet it is when Heaven approves
What nature likes to do!

A happy boy was Frank indeed,
As he may guess who chooses,
His pennies from the spoiler freed,
His body safe from bruises.

He uttered ne'er a word at all,
But merely gazed at Jim,
And bought some apples at a stall,
And gave them all to him.

So Jimmy marches on with pride,
  A fighting-cock of feather,
And Frankie hobbles at his side,—
  And home they go together.

What need to chronicle the joy
  Of mother and of sisters,
Enraptured to behold their boy
  Preserved from wounds and blisters!

They kissed and kissed his tiny face,
  Each jealous of the other;
Then took brave Jimmy into grace
  And made him son and brother.

They feasted him with choicest fare,
  And on their warmest bed
The lad (half wondering if he dared)
  Reposed his ragged head.

* * * *

Some weeks passed pleasantly, the same
  In peace and happy stillness.
At length a great misfortune came,
  For Frank was seized with illness.

And Jimmy, sad to say, was bound
  To leave the homely dwelling,
Wherein, poor fellow, he had found
  A joy too great for telling.

* * * *

Now whether Frankie lived or died,
  I know not which the way be,—
Nor will I wander without guide
  Through regions of the may-be;

For whether Frank be here or there—
  In earth or heaven above—
He lives within the holy care
  Of God, and God is Love.

But as for Jimmy, I have heard
  That, after many changes,
Much flight, like Noah's sable bird,
  O'er waste and weary ranges,

A friendly hand was tow'rds him spread
  By one of Mercy's daughters,
Who called the vagrant thing, and shed
  Across the troubled waters

The radiance of celestial love,
Which beamed upon this raven,
And gave him plumage of the dove,
And lit him to a haven

Where hellish tempests do not come.
To speak more plain and fairly,
Rough Jimmy now has found a home,
And work that suits him rarely.

A fiery work of power and pith—
Oh! livelier far than tillage—
Rough Jim is now the stoutest smith
That ever wrought in village.

And, glorying in his might of hand,
When merry-makings come,
Most jovial of the village Band
He thunders on the drum.

Farewell, friend readers: oh! believe,
There is no better fashion
Of giving, that ye may receive
God's bounties of compassion

Along with store of sweet delights,
  Than helping in the labours
Of those who save our Ishmaelites
  And make them honest neighbours.

PART III.

DAY-SPRING.

IN the gray of the dawn I dreamt a dream,
    In the ghastly hour when day draws nigh,
When morning smiles with a sickly gleam
And leaden clouds go creeping by.

I dreamt that my life was shorn of its gloss,
That the only glow of my life was gone,
That its sweetest gain was whelmed in loss,
That its latest light of joy had shone.

I dreamt that my love lay low in her shroud,
With her face like the moon-white marble still:
Then I woke from my dream, and I cried aloud,
And my tears went forth as the rush of a rill.

And hellish fiends on my spirit trod,
And they mocked and taunted, and laughed me
    to scorn:
'Ho! this is the man that trusted in God;
Better for him had he never been born.

'Better to dwell in the deeps of the dark
As an embryo nestled in nature's womb,
Than to rise at the touch of the mystic spark
And wander through light into uttermost gloom.

'What is that life which thou prizest so well,
But a reptile's writhe, on the granite cast;
A helpless crawl to a nameless hell,
The grave of thy loves and of thee at last?

'True was thy dream as the wisdom of old
On souls prophetic in vision shed:
Thy love's fair body for ever is cold,
Her spirit for ever and ever is dead.

'Yea! do our boding voices lie?
Were thy senses mocked by a jest or a play?
Yet doom is certain, and death is nigh,
Though it lag for a decade, or come in a day.

'Dreams are the mirrored forms of things
Which Fate's dim treasuries garnered keep,
And Night's gray messenger deftly brings
The image of truth to a dweller in sleep.

'Lo, time is a scorn to him that sees
Both whence it issues and whither it tends,
'Tis a billow that rises, and breaks, and flees,
And sinks in the ocean and finds its end.

'Ever the all-world ocean has flowed,
Ever the all-world ocean flows;
And it surges on as its fates may bode,
Nor love, nor mercy, nor justice knows.

'What is that God which thou fain wouldst seek?
What is that heaven where thou fain wouldst be?
Ask of the winds austere and bleak,
Ask of the bitter barren sea:

'Ask of the lurid lightning fire;
Of the putrid plague that stalks from the fen;
Ask of the desert monsters dire
That waste and ravage the world of men.

'Up with thy voice, O fool, and shout
Curse upon curse, till thy brain whirls round:
Then snatch at the steel, and thy life let out;—
So shall thy sleep be calm and sound!'

But I fell on my knees and I wrestled in prayer,
As Israel wrestled till break of day ;
And I fought so hard in my stark despair
That the angel never could give me nay.

And sometimes I spoke, and I sometimes wept
And silently lifted my heart on high ;
Till the passion wearied and waned and slept,
And my pulses faltered and seemed to die.

Then a balm on my innermost being was poured,
And it soothed as a kindly father's kiss ;
And I knew that I lay in the light of the Lord,—
And 'twas partly sorrow and partly bliss—

For I feebly felt that a woe was there,
But the cause could not trouble my lovely rest ;
I wished not a wish and I breathed not a prayer,
For my will was God's, and his will was best.

And my spirit chanted a holy song :
'God is Truth and Beauty and Love.
Let thy soul be glad and thy heart be strong,
Though the days be short, or the days be long,
In earth below, or heaven above.'

SONG TO AZRAEL.

ANGEL of death! Serene and gentle being!
When shall I gaze on thy mildly gleaming brow!
When, lovely angel, shall I with thee be fleeing
Far from the weariness that grieves my spirit now!
Far from all the weariness,
Far from all the heaviness,
Far from all the wretchedness,
That grieve my spirit now.

Once I did hate thee, loving pure-eyed angel,
Thought thee the frown of an angry, cruel God;
Feared thee, yet dared thee, yet cursed thee, blessêd angel,—
Cursing and daring thee, yet cowering at thy rod:
Hating thee in bitterness,
Braving thee in recklessness,
Daring thee in haughtiness,
Yet cowering at thy rod.

Angel of death! Sweet paradisal lily!
I love thee, thou harbinger of joys assured for aye.
What though the river be deep and dark and chilly,
Safe thou wilt carry me to everlasting day.
Angel of true friendliness,
Angel of mild-heartedness,
Bear me with all speediness
To everlasting day!

ROSE AND IVY.

COLD ivy broods on yonder cottage wall,
And, as a dragon spreads her wings of blight,
Its mournful masses form a shadowy pall
That canopies the stone with dreary night.
Yet through the foliage make resistless way
Soft crimson flowerets of a tender rose,
Which, pining for sweet air and light of day,
Clean past that tyrannous oppression goes.

Soul without hope of happiness, arise!
Press through the barriers wrought by hands abhorred;
Up from thy dungeon! toil thou, agonise
To reach the comfort of thy spirit's Lord:
Forth, darkened soul! from earth to lights above,
And sun thy sorrow in the rays of Love.

CLEAR VISION.

THE day will come when thou shalt see
The spirit hosts that round thee wait;
Not in this lifetime shall it be,
But in thy dis-embodied state.

For could thine eyes e'en once discern
The forms of horror thronging near,
Thy soul to joy would ne'er return,
Distraught with sorrow, wonder, fear.

And midst them pass the spirits pure,
Of essence fine and formless grace,
Thy gentle friends, thy guardians sure;
The shivering demons yield them place.

But cease to yearn for sights above,
And bend thine eyes to sights below;
Live out the life of patient love,
Mourn less thine own, than others', woe.

ASPIRATION.

O Lord, Thou art so good,
My spirit weak and rude
Desires from out the dust its weary self to raise:
Lord, lift me from the gloom
That holds me in the tomb,
And teach me how to smile, and teach me how to praise.

Thou blest immortal King,
The praises I can sing
Are all unworthy Thee to hearken to and hear;
For we indeed are nought
But wretched creatures, fraught
With earthliness and guilt, and doubtfulness and fear.

Send forth Thy blessêd power
And aid me, hour by hour,
To battle with the foes that haunt my mortal frame;
Send influence from on high,
That ere this body die
My soul may win the light of purest heavenly flame.

DREAM LINES.

ALONE, upon my bed I lie,
The blessêd spirits come and go :
I see them, not with outward eye,
My heart beats still and low.

Softly the peaceful spirits glide,
As snow that falls undriven,
They throng around on every side
And show the steps to Heaven—
Bright as the light these steps abide,
From heavenly quarries riven.

Then drawn as by a magnet force,
For rapturous hours my soul floats free,
And follows on the boundless course
Of the angel company.

Ah ! when my being sends her breath
To roam in happy, heavenly ways,—
It is not life, it is not death :
The mystery of endless praise.

A SONG OF CHEER.

COME to the power that will teach thee to sing
Strains that the breezes of Paradise bring;
Open thy being to floods of the grace
Poured from the founts of the mystical place!

Where are the pleasures that pall not at last?
Where are the climes that are safe from the blast?
Wouldst thou be happy and peaceful and blest,
Trust in the Lord, with a conscience at rest.

Cease to be woful and weary of mood,
Live in the strength of the Spirit of good,
Keep thou from sinning and live thou secure,
Angels are many in homes of the pure.

List to the songs of the birds of the grove,
Sweet with contentment and merry with love;
Love makes an Eden for innocent things,
Evil unknowing and agile of wings.

Man cannot sing with the songs of a bird—
Sin has a cadence that ever is heard,—
Pure though his soul in its uttermost choice,
Conscience is his, and it clings to his voice.

Nay then, in Heaven thou shalt have for thine own
Music more mellow in measure and tone;
Birds may the echoes of Eden prolong,
Glorified souls in themselves are a song.

A PARABLE.

AS bees to some fair solitude
Wing their swift way in search of food,
But straight return, and zealous strive
To swell the treasures of the hive:
Thus do thou, man of God!—repair
To solitude; to mountains, where
The holy breaths of Heaven are rushing;
Or to the darksome forest, hushing
The heart with awe ecstatic,—there
Diffuse thy very self in prayer.
Then fed with beauty from above
Proceed thou, fraught with hope and love,
To share the tainted ugliness
Of peopled haunts, where myriads press,
Enthralled by work; while some reclining,
Hell-fettered, know not they are pining;
Feed their starved souls with Eden sweetness—
Unmeasured got, but given with meetness;—

So shall thy spirit lighted be
From lovely lamps of Sympathy.

He who would feast the multitude
Must first win wealth of Heavenly food:
Heaven's food devoured, and not imparted,
Makes the lone feaster sorry-hearted.

SPIRIT MUSIC.

MAN toils and schemes for wealth and glory;
But they alone can compass joy
Who mystically mark the story
Of love, too heavenly pure to cloy;

Which breathes a music echoing faintly
The blissful melody of souls,
That rings around the mansions saintly
And o'er the crystal ocean rolls, -

A melody that moves and trances
Though measureless its accents be,
For Nature's spirit sings and dances
In cadence with its harmony.

And where no human sounds are stirring
In woodland or on mountain heights,
The lovely music, oft recurring,
Will yield its delicate delights

To souls attuned to feel it thrilling
  Above the voices desert-born
Of breeze, and brook, and song-burst trilling
  From creatures lone and sweetly lorn.

Yet murmur of the crowds that welter
  In sordid cities vilely pent,
Whom vampire pinions shade and shelter
  And fan into a false content,

Hath sounds of Heaven within its moaning,
  And notes of pleasant Paradise,—
While cadenced to the fitful groaning
  Of dwellers under evil skies;

For, hovering o'er the vocal drearness
  Begot of cynic worldly song,
Arise glad notes of angel clearness
  From holy haunters of the throng.

Though body dwell 'mid graves and gutters
  In darksome dens where fiends rejoice,
A heavenly soul high music utters
  And climbs to Eden on its voice;

Or on that lovely lucent ladder
  The angel comforters descend,
And gladder grows the soul, and gladder,
  Till gladness come that cannot end.

Yea, though, 'mong fiends more foul of savour,
  In courtly homes the body stay,
A sacred soul will gently quaver
  As birds that sing in autumn's gray.

Sad, sad its chant among the hazes
  Of fog-benighted worldly air;
Yet moves it singing through the mazes,
  Till Heaven is found, and rapture there.

THE CHOSEN CASKET.[24]

MIGHT of the many-mouthêd throng
Resplendent in the realms of day,
Attend, and glorify my song,
Invigorate the words I say.

Appear, ye holy hosts, that wait
Around the adamantine throne,
That celebrate the high estate
Of Him who reigns—who reigns alone.

Come, strike with me the mystic strain
Of one whose life was orderêd
In days long past, when Afric's main
Was not,—nor Nile's wide waters led,

Tremendous, where the Egyptian Sphinx
In subtle silence lurks and broods,
And knows the mystery that links
Proud manhood and the purple woods.

There was a man, in days thus old,
Who swayed the realms with magic force,—
The waters in his hand could hold,
Could stay the tempest's lurid course;

Could hurl the mountain from its base,
And on the many-fountained sea
Could wrap a measureless embrace
And hold it as with lock and key;

For neither tide, nor billowy rush
Of waves impelled by wintry storm,
Could brook the all-commanding hush
Proceeding from that potent form,

Who ruled the sons of men with spells
Born in the cavern of the height,
Where many a spirit that rebels
Remains concealed in solemn night;

And from their lips he gained a word
So potent in its magic power
That e'en the vast celestial bird
Would leave its eyrie, in the hour

That love imperious claimed its stay
To murmur with its pleasant mate,
And through the æther haste away
To meet the summons, strong as fate,

Resounding in its inner ears,—
So low, yet mystically loud,
That nought that once that cadence hears
Can think to make its heart so proud

As risk the torments that portend
For all who listen to that note
And will not to its bidding bend,—
Its cry that creeps from shores remote,

Its all-embracing cooing cry,
So ghastly sweet, so fiendly sour,
The essence of that harmony
Which blends in one the demon-power

Opposed to God—whose single glance
Could yet annihilate their might,
And pierce them with a fiery lance
Of His own life's essential light.

The man who bore this magic spell
(Concealed in mystery of forms,
Designéd to hide what none should tell
Of that slow heat whose radiance warms

The very source of conscious life)
This man believed that only he
Might rule the earth, his soul was rife
With hate and scorn and blasphemy.

He dwelt alone, within a fort
Hewn from the solid granite rock,—
To which the devils oft resort,
In hopes to hide them from the shock

Of some dire stroke of punishment
Decreed to check some grievous deed:
But angels as avengers sent
No forts of stubborn granite heed;

On, on they rush, and with a sweep
Of their tremendous wings of fire
They hurl the devils to the deep,
And rack them with th' Almighty's ire.

The evil man sat day by day
Within his lonesome mountain-cave;
His cruel mind devised its play
In spreading woes that fill the grave,—

The foul corroding pestilence
That eats a nation's flesh and blood,
The mental blight that blasts the sense
And whelms the spirit like a flood.

The earth would open at his call,
And gape in ghastly sulphurous pits;
Would belch out flaming fires on all
Possessed of aught that counterfeits

The joys of Heaven in earthly bliss.
He hated joy that was not sin,
And where man's spirit met not his
He quelled the flesh it homed within.

He lived in bestial revelry.
All joys that minister to sense
He seized. He wallowed in the sea
Of filthiness, whose tides immense

Lap sluggish on the endless shore
Of putrid, festering, reeking ooze,—
Which bounds the land, for evermore,
Assigned to spirits that refuse

To hear the solemn conscience-voice
That whispers soft or thunders high,
And, God-defying, make their choice
To hate the Truth and love the Lie.

Now in the land where reigned this king
(For king he was, as mortals deem,)
There bloomed in sweetest blossoming
A maiden,—lovely as the dream

That dances in the soul of one
Whom angels visit in the night,
And through his quivering pulses run
The ecstasies of still delight;—

So fair was she, so gently fair,
As melody's meandering rill
When tenderest music haunts the air
And breezes to its kisses thrill.

Her form was of that sacred mould
Which, in the ages of the prime,
When earth was young (that now is old),
Beamed on the eyes of new-born time:

So calmly strong, so nobly sweet;
So lofty, yet so lowly mild;
All Heavenly glories seemed to meet
To glorify a Heavenly child.

This lovely maiden oft would seek
The treasures of the early morn,—
The dews that glitter on the cheek
Of Nature's tender younglings, born

So softly fair that none would deem
How flowerets of such dainty form
Could e'er be strengthened to beteem
The fury of the drifting torm;—

And as one morn, beneath the rays
Shed by the sun in golden showers,
She wandered through the leafy bays
And gathered store of beauteous flowers,

It chanced that he of evil mind—
The foul magician called a king—
Passed prowling through the groves, behind
The place where she was wandering.

And as she went upon her way,
His eye accursêd marked her grace:
He doomed her to become the prey
That his vile passion-hounds should chase.

He turned him round and met the maid,
And fixed on her an eye of might,
And spells so dreadful o'er her laid
She felt no thoughts of wrong or right,

Of terror, or of cònfidence;
But in a silent trance amazed,
She waited,—nor had moved her thence
Had lightning flashes round her blazed.

The cursêd one approached her near,
He cast his arms around her waist
And whispered mystery in her ear;
Then bared the beauty of her breast,

And printed there a potent seal,
Too strong for aught on earth to move,—
A pledge that nothing should reveal
The secret of his cruel love.

Then forth he went, and she with him;
His steps her faltering steps pursued,
While in her slumbered, darkly dim,
The life and light of maidenhood.

They neared the tower of granite build.
Lo! on the threshold moaned forlorn
A little babe, whose eyes distilled
Gray pearls of grief,—as newly-born

Will weep and wail to leave the home
Wherein their embryo being lay,
Through earth's old darknesses to roam
Lamenting for the vanished day.

The wizard fixed his evil eye
On that poor infant at his gate:
Ferocious glimmers rise, and fly
To blast with overpowering hate

The thing so innocent and mean
That dares to linger in his sight;
And on his glances fiends obscene
Ride wildly, bearing baneful blight.

Then onward steps he; and, with heel
Of one that crushes reptiles flat,
He thinks to make the infant feel
Strong pains of anguish. Lo, a bat

Comes flitting past, and shrilly cries—
'O fool of fools! the thing to scorn
Is not the babe that helpless lies,
But he, who—ere the light of morn

'Has made the movement of a span
From eastern womb to western grave—
Will cease to tread the haunts of man,
Will learn the terrors of the cave.'

Then broke a thunder on the air,
As when a host of chariots sweep
Across the battlefield, and bear
Their scythèd blades, that swiftly reap

The cowering crops of daunted men,
And dew the stubbled plain with blood.
It comes—it comes—it comes again—
With roarings of a river flood,

That bursts upon the shaking rocks—
Unmeet to moderate its force—
And whirls them with resistless shocks
Down the wild terrors of its course!

And from the forehead of the child
A light as clear as crystal came,
His azure eyes with radiance smiled,
And splendour covered all his frame:

And from his mouth there went a sword
As piercing pure as spirit-fire;
Its light enwrapt the evil lord,
And scorched him with its tongues of ire.

He sank, and grovelled on the ground,
And strove to speak his mightiest spell:
The fetid demons crowded round;
But fearful anguish on them fell;

And all the air was filled with flames,
And through the fire came angel hands,—
And voices spake the demon's names,
And straightway they were marked with brands,

To tell to all the spirit-race
That the enchanter's cursêd crew
Were stigmatised with such disgrace
As falls on crime of deadliest hue,

Were thenceforth to be held as those
Degraded even from the lot
Of such as sometimes find repose,—
For, seeking, these would find it not.

Then rose the child, and all his frame
Expanded in the might of God;
Broad beams of fire around him came,
And formed an incandescent road,

On which there went a spirit host
Bedecked with jewelled armour bright,—
The sheen of rubies shone from most,
And many moved in azure light,

And others showed the changeful hues
Of emerald charged with lunar beams,—
And others sparkled like the dews
Of Eden, as the diamond gleams.

And all this glory-bearing crowd
Sang praises with a mighty voice,
Till the gray mountains echoed loud,
As if the desert would rejoice.

Low sank the maiden on her knees,
Full fraught with rapture and with pain;
But he—the child—now lord of these
Who brought such beauty in their train,

Placed holy hand upon her brow,
And decked her with the light of Heaven;
And all the angels round her bow,
To whom such majesty is given.

Then from the all-exalted King
Proceeds a high creative word;
Whereat the angels, wondering
At the transcendent voice they heard,

Shivered and trembled, and their forms
Threw glistening gleams of fiery bloom,
As when the meteor sons of storms
Illuminate a sultry gloom.

Then further spake the King,—'Pure maid,
Of spirit clearer than the day,
The power of God is on thee laid,
And grace shall ever with thee stay.

'And from thee shall a son arise
Whose name shall o'er the earth be spread:
To him shall all men lift their eyes
For help to raise them from the dead.

'Till the appointed season come
When man shall know this holy grace,
Abide thou in a Heavenly home,—
The river-girdled resting-place.'

He spake: and glory round her swept,
And seraphs bore her to the land
Where long she lay, and silent slept,
With golden guards at either hand.

FATHERLY COUNSEL.

O Thou, my son! my wan day's evening star,—
The path of life stands wide and opens far
Before thy youthful eyes; for me the grave
Gapes greedy: O my child, I fain would save
Thy fair young soul from sorrow's cruel pang,
Would guide thee to the bliss that angels sang—
Peace,—that sweet peace which in God's favour lies,
Peace in this world and peace in Paradise.

Brief be my task to bid thee shun the crowd
From good apostate and to evil vowed,
With such to class thee were a stigma thrown
On honest blood, thy mother's and my own;
More need to warn thee from the foolish throng
Who hope to rise to right through doing wrong,
Who, prayerless, fain would thrive on others' prayers,
And think to reap Heaven's grain by sowing tares.
And yet, to heed their talk, what wisdom lies
In all the store of mean apologies

Which for their lips a crafty demon brings,—
Bloat Belial whispering under angel's wings!
'Behold,' say such, 'how from a rake's reform
The fairest sainthood springs, as shine from storm;
By chance, or grace, such glory I may win,
Gain future crowns, yet live in present sin.
Ah yes, I know that death, with sudden gripe,
May blight me ere my heavenly fruit be ripe;
And then beyond reprieve my lot were Hell:
But why suppose the worst, where none can tell?'
O senseless ones! like simple calves that play
In groves where lions, roaring, roam for prey,
To prove your risks unwise, no need to school
My son, whom none can designate a fool:
But wisdom's very self will often fail
To spy out falsities beneath the veil
Of sacred jargon which too long has decked
The savage bareness of some ancient sect.
My son, my son! if man, or fiend, or book,
Shall say, or seek to say, that God will look
On sin, as on a spice that serves for good
As previous zest to flavour gospel food;
That faith, repentance, saintliness, will draw
So thick a covering over former flaw,
That sin's deep damage will no more be seen,
Its wounds healed scarless, washed and plaistered clean;—

Go tell that book, that demon, or that man,
To keep such talk for those unfit to scan
That sentence which the world's wide face displays,
In present times as in the earlier days :—
'What 's right is right : e'en so, what 's wrong is wrong,
(Though sirens gainsay with seductive song) ;
Nor strength resides in Heaven's own boundless might
To make one right a wrong, one wrong a right.'
Found not false hopes upon Salvation-blood
Shed o'er the world in sin-expunging flood,
(No thought of mine to cavil at the Cross,
Let me but free good gold from sordid dross) ;
Pains may be lessened, strength o'er weakness cast,
But none can e'er annihilate a past.
Say, ye who deem that every truth resides
Within one book, Heaven's truth and nought besides,
By what strange instinct do ye learn to dart—
As bees on flowers—upon some fragrant part?
While others—fragrant too, of tenderest bloom—
Are left to sicken in their own perfume?
Wherefore forget the white-robed virgin band
Who in God's open presence alway stand?
Why fail to mark pure infancy's chief grace—
'Their angels aye behold the Father's face'?
Nay; search the sacred book from end to end,
And nought but prejudice can apprehend

That in mere pardon farther magic dwells
Than in mere rescue from the nether Hells;
Or that the Prodigal, though welcomed home,
Stands high as he who never sought to roam.
The penitent of heart whose earthly days
The Lord prolongs, perchance may learn to raise
His sunken soul to glories and to powers
Beyond the reach of some, whose placid hours,
Unmarked by lofty deeds or loathsome crime,
Have felt no ripple of the sea of time;
Yet, shall not those by desperate evil scarred,
To all eternity be found debarred
From that close access to the All-pure's throne
Reserved for crime-unsullied souls alone?
Or shall sunk souls, whatever grace conferred,
E'er stand as high as if they ne'er had erred?
I know not,—none can know,—yet all may look,
Where Scriptures speak not, on the open book
Of man's own heart, in primal impulse given
By no snake-tempter, but by holy Heaven;
There learn what e'en an earthly sire may feel,
Who as his friend would greet the deadly steel,
If for a daughter his own life might buy
Escape from loss of virgin purity;
Yet who, though sin had all her honour wrecked,
A mourning penitent would ne'er reject,

But clasp her to his pardoning breast, and prove
That still for her remained a father's love :—
A father's love—but could e'en that restore
The maiden-glory gone for evermore ?

My son, my son ! walk thou with God secure,
True, gentle, valiant, and as maiden pure ;
Let no seductive arts, nor ridicule,
Of tainted traitor or of empty fool,
No sickly senseless craving to excel
Bravado-sliders down the slope of Hell,
Once o'er thy reasoning brain a glamour cast,
Hide the grand future and the peaceful past,
And lead thee—reft of will, and wit, and all
That makes man more than brute—to sudden fall
From peace to trouble, joy to gnawing pain,
With loss eternities can ne'er regain.
Fear not, my son, the ridicule of those
Whose wits are like the fitful gale that blows
Hard northern blights, then straightway shifts its mouth,
And sheds forth softness from the genial south.
Let each poor Boreas mock and roar and rave,
Stand firm, my son, be patient and be brave ;
Soon will that blast abate ; perhaps, indeed,
Blow sweetness : should it not, yet wherefore heed ?

Boyhood is short, and the well-ripened man
Will praise in thee what once he dared to ban,
Will mourn the past, its wrongs will seek to mend,
Will strive to make of thee an honoured friend.

Right well I know that, in these things I ask,
I offer thee a hard and bitter task;
'Tis irksome bondage to abide by rule,
Stings lurk in laughter of the veriest fool.
Yet, were this all the obstacle that stands
To bar thy progress to celestial lands,
Glad would I cry—'Fear nought, go seize the crown!
Press onward, spur thy sloth, laugh laughter down!'
Alas, ere many a year hath made its flight,
Thy soul will need to arm itself for fight,
With helmet, sword, and shield, more strong than those
By common force employed 'gainst common foes.
For, when the wheels of war most fiercely roll,
Then wilt thou find arch-traitors in thy soul,
Strong-voiced to bid thee play a recreant part
And clasp sin's comfort to thy fevered heart.
Ah, my dear son, in those thrice-dangerous hours
Trust not for victory to thy native powers;
'Gainst passion's force what weapon may prevail?
Thoughts, vows, hopes, wishes,—all are like to fail.

Nay then, my son, no reason to despair;
One aid remains, the potent aid of pray'r:
Prayer, that good weapon framed for use conjoint,—
Breastplate and helm, as well as edge and point.
Prayer-swords glint gleams which flashing upward go,
Hurled back as Heaven's dread lightning on the foe.
Yes, prayer is great; and he who heeds not pray'r
Risks more than mortal may presume to dare:
Yes, prayer is great; but not alone for use
When, round thee, fiends of hell are raging loose;
Prayer is a thing for every purpose good,
For feast celestial, or for daily food;—
A balm for sorrow, and a zest for joy;
A moment's solace, or an hour's employ;
A solemn sacrifice on bended knee,
The speechless groan of utmost agony;
The strong ejaculation swiftly sent,
The frameless whisper of a sweet content;
The mingling voice of many Heav'nward thrown,
The secret sigh of one with God alone.
Prayer is the cherub that exultant brings
Man's noblest needs before the King of kings;
Prayer is the seraph that indulgent flies
To bear man's feeblest crave to sacred skies:
In work or play, in happiness or care,
Mix prayer with every thought, and thought with pray'r.

Belovèd one! all joys for me below
Glad would I forfeit, could my soul but know
That my dear child, his earthly course outrun,
Would shine for ever, a resplendent sun,
Rich in the glory God confers on those
Who, not content with bafflement of foes
Through steadfastness to struggle and withstand,
Have carried war into the hostile land,
Great wrongs redressed, truth's banner wide unfurled,
Displayed a light to re-illume the world,—
Light fed with heavenly oil, abundant poured
From the exhaustless vessels of the Lord,
The human radiance privileged to shine
Through closest union with the light divine.
Alas for man, such glories few attain:
Scarce dare I hope that thou that crown wilt gain.
Yet, failing there (thy spirit found too weak),
This much, in God's great name, I charge thee seek—
Seek with each atom of thy striving soul,
With prayers that like an ocean's pulses roll,—
That God will grant thee, at the hour of death,
To raise this song with thy last sigh of breath:—
'Great Lord of Heaven, I thank Thee for the grace
That calls me nearer to Thy Holy Place.
Through countless perils Thou hast brought me in,
And kept my soul from taint of deadly sin.

No boast, O Lord, from these poor lips shall fall;
My strength was nothing, but Thy strength was all:
No praise I claim, no merit count mine own,
My hope is rested on Thy grace alone,—
That grace which prompts me to exulting praise,
While all my faults are open to Thy gaze.
Hear, then, ye friends who stand around this bed,
Hear the last words of one about to tread
The shores of death:—Throughout my earthly time,
Ne'er have I felt the shadow of a crime;
In age, in manhood, childhood, and in youth,
Ne'er have I failed to act and speak the truth;
Ne'er from the paths of pureness have I erred,—
Pure have I lived, in thought, in deed, in word.
No cruel action have I ever done;
Ne'er wronged, reviled, or slandered any one.
Love have I shown to all. My faults forgiven,
I go to join the Family of Heaven.'

IN MEMORY OF G. H. D.[25]

OB. DEC. 2, 1875.

I.

AS when o'er wastes of wild Saskátchewan
  Fast bound in manacles of frost and snow,
A weary wayworn wanderer struggles on,
  Faint, famished, bleeding, hope nigh lost—and lo!
Dear friends surround him, raise him in their arms;
  And, ere his palsied sense can comprehend
The greatness of his gain, he feels the charms
  Of warmth and rest with all his being blend:—
Thus struggles, faints, despairs, a parting soul
  Emerging from its chrysalis of clay,
Alone and agonised; when straight uproll
  The spirit-veils, and there in golden day
Smiles each sweet heav'n-born friend of earth's old love:
Love dies not in the tomb, it lives and blooms above.

II.

As when the high Soldan, in the mystic East,
  Through faithful messengers hath heard repute
Of one serenely good, and fain would feast
  His eyes on him, and sendeth forth a mute
To bring the man unwarned; and he, aghast,
  Falls prostrate, dreading doom through stern decree;
And off they drag his garb;—but lo! they cast
  Upon his shoulder robes of majesty:—
Thus 'tis with thee, O friend of happy days!
  O man of charity and genial worth!
Thy garb of sorrow changed for robes of praise,
  To deck the soul resplendent in new birth.
True friend of many friends! when, dazed and bare,
We reach the unseen realms, ah! speed to meet us there.

PART IV.

GREENWOOD'S FAREWELL.

OLD Greenwood lay a-dying :—
His sons beside him stand,
His dog is near him lying,
His daughter holds his hand.

His parish priest, true-hearted,
Still strives, with anxious care,
To fix his soul, ere parted,
To Heavenly thought and prayer.

His life was slowly waning ;
His voice, though low and weak,
Gave without pause or straining
The words he chose to speak.

'Dear boys,' he feebly uttered,
'I cannot bear the gloom
Of this dull den, half-shuttered ;
Come, take me to my room—

'The room I used to stay in,
That looks upon the park;
To drink some light of day in,
Before my eyes grow dark.'

Each turned, and sought to gather
Advice from each one's brow:
The daughter said—'Dear father,
We fear to move you now.'

A few sad tears escape her:
Said he, 'My child, I doubt
This poor old flickering taper
Is soon to be put out:

'It matters not what moment
The fateful hand may fall;
Last hours are not for woe meant,
But for good-byes to all.'

'Ah!' said the parson, 'truly
Prolonged last hours afford,
To those that use them duly,
Much cause to praise the Lord.

'Prayer doth the spirit brighten,
And time is given for prayers;
Thought doth the cords untighten
That bind to earthly cares:

'And oft in that blest season,
Ere parts the failing breath,
Come angels;—hence the reason
We shrink from sudden death.

'Waste not, dear friend, the hours
God gives; I pray thee pause,
Nor tax thy failing powers
For aught but solemn cause.'

The old man smiled, half sadly,
And half with feeble glee;
Said he—'You argue badly,
As any one might see.

'For how can your resistance
To all for which I strive,
Be of such great assistance
In keeping me alive?

'And when did you discover
The adage less than true—
Be rid of the old lover
Ere taking on the new?

'I can't well wish, nor dare well,
To meet the King of Kings,
Until I 've looked my farewell
On pleasant earthly things.

'Come, come, my boys! don't dally,
But bear me up like men
In your stout arms; we 'll sally
From this lugubrious den.'

They raised him up, and wrapped him
In silken dressing-gown,
With soft black velvet capped him,
And then they bore him down.

Bright Harold raised his shoulder,
And Richard raised his knee,
In front walked Edwin, older;
'Twas thus they went all three.

Old Greenwood smiled a smile, as
He passed his daughter near :
'Ianthe, keep friend Silas
A little while up here'—

(He whispered low) : 'that parson
With looks so grave and wise—
His coat alone would bar sun
From shining o'er one's eyes.

'So keep him with you, sweetest ;
But not too long, my pet,
For Time runs best and fleetest
When he has prey to get.'

Her eyes smiled sad, like moonbeams
That flicker cold in caves ;
Then gleamed with love, as noon beams
O'er lilies grown on graves.

She kissed his broad white forehead,
And stroked his locks of gray :
Then from that room abhorrèd
They carried him away,

Along the passage vaulted,
And down the wide stone stair;
Till in his room they halted,
And placed him in the chair

Where oft he sat and pondered,
Before his strength decayed,
And watched the deer that wandered
Across the ferny glade.

He sank down, still and pallid—
They thought he 'd gone to rest,—
Then set his teeth and rallied,
And proudly raised his crest.

'Nay, Master Worm,' he muttered,
'I 'm not yet meat for thee!
Why look ye, lads, so fluttered?
See, Edwin, take this key,

'And bring the little phial
You 'll find in yon oak case—
Though Death won't take denial,
The knave shall wait a space!'

He drinks. A sudden crisis—
It does not last for long.
Behold his colour rises,
His voice comes free and strong.

Said he—'That sly Italian
Professed to work by spell—
The conjuring rascallion!—
Yet this has served me well.

'Oh how my spirits dance! I—
Dear boys, don't think me queer—
I feel the strangest fancy
To go and shoot a deer.

'Yes, yes, I quite remember—
The shooting season 's o'er,
We 're almost in November:
Ha! there 's the old stag's roar.

'Push, push my chair in nearer,
And thrust aside the blinds;
I want to see him, clearer,
Rush raving round his hinds.

'Ah, there he is! Good-bye, lad,
Heaven keep thee stout and bold
For many a day—while I, lad,
Am rotting in the mould.

'But stay—no time to trifle,
There still is much to do—
Boys, reach me down my rifle,
And hold it in my view.

'The beautiful old barrels!
What finely tapering grace!
How soft the light apparels
Their veined and clouded face!

'Belovêd fellow-sharer
Of all my happiest hours,
Years make thee but the fairer,
And weaken not thy powers:

'While I—to me Time's rigour
Has dealt such grievous harms,
I find not even vigour
To bear thee in mine arms.

'How many a beast thy bullet
Hath robbed of vital breath!
Thy trigger—could I pull it,
To save myself from death?

'What whirl of memory centres
On this companion true!'—
(Here Mr. Silas enters,
Ianthe enters too.)

'Those pleasant Scottish mountains!
Those fragrant, blooming heights!
Mine eyes might well be fountains
To weep the past delights,

'When, o'er my senses crowded,
All sweetnesses would blend:
Soon shall I lie enshrouded; —
And then?'—'Alas, dear friend,'

Said Silas, 'fix your eye on
The Heavenly crystal sea,
The fair celestial Zion.'
Said Greenwood—'Why to me

'Discourse of lands ideal,
Where mortal man ne'er roved?
The seen, the known, the real—
The utterly beloved,

'So satisfies my spirit
I'd yield my right-of-birth
To all that saints inherit,
If I might stay on earth.'

'Prefer a "mess of pottage,"
Said Silas, 'to the bread
Of Heaven—like Esau's dotage?
Bethink thee!' 'I have said,'—

The other answered slowly;
''Twere easy to assent
To all that sounds most holy;
But surely punishment,

'Not honour, would attend on
Such weak untruthful slips:
Strange deed to urge one's friend on
To die with lying lips!

'But stay—thou wilt not flatter?—
One thing I'd ask of thee—
My thoughts of Heaven less matter—
What are Heaven's thoughts of me?'

A moment's pause succeeded:
Then Silas—'Though 'tis true
Eternity were needed
To work that problem through,

'Yet let me tell thee briefly,
Regarding God's high thought,
In God's own nature chiefly
Thine answer must be sought;

'Not 'mong all abstract notions
In the Almighty mind,
(We plumb not such deep oceans),
But, to that part confined

'Which, His own Church revealing,
No man may disallow;
'Tis thus we'll judge His feeling
Tow'rds you, dear friend, just now.

'First, let us view Tradition,
In every phase;—sublime'—
Said Greenwood: 'With submission,
Let 's choose some other time.'

Said Silas: 'Nay, my dear friend,
I meant not far to stray.
Glad tidings of good cheer, friend,
Be thine without delay.

'To one like thee, devoted
To Holy Church from youth,
Whom nought hath e'er denoted
Inclined to lapse from truth;

'Whose conscience doth not labour
In bonds of deadly sin;
Who never wronged his neighbour,
But served him as his kin;

'No prodigal, while living
To suit his rank and state;
Most bountiful in giving;
One ever temperate

' In pleasures of the senses ;
Who kept in due control
His temper ; all offences
Who pardoned from his soul ;

' Kind father, friend, and master :
I say to such a one—
Death brings not thee disaster ;
Be of good cheer, my son.'

He ended. Solemn stillness
A while pervades the room,
Then Greenwood—' 'Tis the chillness
Prophetic of the tomb,

' Perhaps, that daunts my spirits ;
For, spite of all you 've said
Regarding my poor merits,
I feel, within, like lead.

' No errors of behaviour
Much on my conscience prey ;
I know there is a Saviour
Who bears our sins away ;

'Oft have I at His altar
Renewed my Christian vow,
Nor need I shrink or falter
To take Communion now.

'Yet there are thoughts that fret me.
Suppose, my sins forgiven,
That God's great grace should let me
Find entry into Heaven:

'Then farewell joy and gladness!
No manly pleasures there;
All psalm-singing and sadness:
The very thought 's despair!

'When, stripped of earthly clothing,
My spirit seeks its place,
I fear this settled loathing
Will drive it into space,

'If not to lowest Hell. Come,
Let 's try this simple test,—
Would any man force welcome
On a reluctant guest?

'Nay, one word more. Assuming
My spirit housed above,
Where, Heaven's own light illuming,
It yet might learn to love

'Things holy: could such learning
Be mine, unless God's heart,
Inspired with tender yearning,
Should make the earlier start

'Tow'rds friendship and affection?
And could He look on me
As fit for such selection,
When nought of sympathy

'For aught in the expansion
Of Heaven in me is found?
Before you build a mansion
You must provide the ground.

'Alas! his destination
'Tis doubtful work to tell,
Who suits no habitation
In either Heaven or Hell.'

Here Greenwood stops,—and closing
His weary, wistful eyes,
Rests like a man half-dozing.
Then Silas slow replies.

—He spoke with some profusion
On various sacred themes;
Yet with a slight confusion,
As one who is, or seems,

Perplexed in reconcilement
Of much-conflicting views;
Unthinking of beguilement,
Yet sedulous to choose

Whate'er might seem to offer
Best hope of quick release
From doubt, whate'er might proffer
Best hope of joy and peace.

He tried Predestination,
Then left it in the lurch;
Then took a firmer station
On doctrines deemed 'High Church';

Then made a brief memorial,
Drawn from the Romish creed,
Of doctrines Purgatorial,—
As comforting indeed

To those whose contemplations
Are dark with dread of Hell:
'Though fiery expiations
Could never serve as well'—

Said he—'from guilt to ease us,
And save from wrath Divine,
As doth the blest Lord Jesus,
Through sacred bread and wine.

'But grant Rome's view excessive'—
Continued he,—'admit
That none should be progressive
Beyond God's Holy Writ;

''Tis not a thing forbidden,
Although with peril fraught,
To search for secrets hidden
In realms of abstract thought,

'Trod by the footprints golden
Of many saintly men,
Of late days,—yea, of olden,
As witness Origen,—

'Who find the word "eternal"
To mean a term that ends,—
E'en for the souls infernal,
Whom God will yet make friends.

'Yea, with divinest measures
All souls the Lord will win—
Through glooms, or pains, or pleasures,
The Lord will bring them in.

'Let teachers dictatorial
Prove ere they disapprove,
Nor blot from Heaven's armorial
Its motto—"God is love."'

Oh! how Ianthe listened,
As by her father's chair
She knelt; her sweet eyes glistened,
For many a tear was there.

'My father,' said the maiden,
And fondly kissed his hand,
'Be not with grief o'erladen;
For ever we shall stand

'Within His blessêd power,
Whose love is now so great:—
Shall death, in one short hour,
Change all that love to hate?'

Old Greenwood, half reviving,
Low murmured—'What is this?
Our lost ones still surviving!
I felt—I felt—her kiss!

'I see!—nay, 'tis my daughter.
Thy mother, dearest child,—
My failing spirit sought her,
In thee methought she smiled.

'Ianthe, when all 's over,
Take the carved ivory box
From out its leathern cover;
Undo the silver locks –

'Remember, love, the pressure
That moves the secret spring,
Within the myrtle tressure
Around the griffin's wing.

'Keep, dearest, all the treasures
That ivory box contains;
Memorials of past pleasures—
Of pleasures and of pains—

'Which, through life's varying weather,
Your mother, dear, and I
Shared lovingly together,
Until she came to die.'

Then spoke they low, concealing
Their words from other ears,
Heart unto heart appealing,
'Midst sighs, and smiles, and tears.

A while good Silas waited,
And, with the brethren three,
In silence contemplated
A scene, which such as he,

Too clerically-minded,
Are apt to underprize ;
(Professionally blinded,
Or twisted in the eyes ;

And, with the best intentions,
Unable to discern,
Beyond the old inventions—
Which served, and serve, their turn

In keeping folk in order,
Who think, talk, pray, or sing,
Within the Christian border,—
Much good in anything ,

As useful to prepare with
For future life, at least :
How serves you aught you share with
The savage and the beast ?).

Though worthy Mr. Silas
Would, on some sudden pinch,
As boldly walk a mile as
His fellow-priests an inch,

Tow'rds nature and fair reason,—
He 'd soon misdoubt himself,
Accuse his wits of treason
And lay them on the shelf.

Thus now the thought distressed him,
That he had soared too high;
Cold conscience-qualms oppressed him:
Suppose his friend should die,

And find his soul provided
With husks instead of bread;
Betrayed, beguiled, misguided,
By him who should have led

The faltering feeble mortal
Into the well-fenced way
That brings to Heaven's bright portal:
Yes, yet he 'd say his say,

Though Hell, its might revealing,
Should fight against each word!—
A truce with human feeling!
God's message must be heard.

He rose, and watched,—restraining
His ardour, keen but cool;
Like a tall heron craning
Above a quiet pool.

His watching soon was over;
Magnetic sympathy
Caused Greenwood to discover
The other's searching eye.

He looked up with a smile, as
He met the parson's gaze;
And said—'Well, Mr. Silas,
You seem in much amaze

'To see my life so lengthened.
To hear my voice so strong.
However I am strengthened
This can't continue long;

'And (as one might be certain)
There are some things to do
Before we drop the curtain
That sees the last act through.'

Said Silas: ''Tis most urgent
To fix your thoughts on Heaven;
To thoughts from thence divergent
Let no more heed be given.'

'Far better die unprayerful,'
Said Greenwood, 'than be shown
For other's good uncareful,
Though careful for one's own.

'While yet my candle's burning,
I've several things to tell
To my dear sons, concerning
These moments of farewell;

'Then to each faithful servant
I next will make bequest;
Then, all my thoughts be fervent
For Heaven and you;—then Rest.'

Good Silas, full of sorrow,
Raised both his hands, and said:
'"To-morrow and to-morrow"—
Ah! Greenwood, some, when dead,

'Will mourn, for bitter reason,
The putting-off Heaven's claim
Till that "convenient season"
Which never, never came.'

'Nay, Silas,' said the other,
'I hope that 's not my case:
I have no wish to smother
My little spark of grace.

'Well—now, my sons, come hither!
My rifle once more bring.
The poor old tree must wither;
But round its ruins spring

'A forest: as Time yellows
The old he greens the new.
My handsome, noble fellows,
I thank the Lord for you!

'My mind no sorrow gathers
From the sad thought which weighs
So heavy on some fathers
About to end their days,—

'That, while the sound yet lingers
Of solemn requiem notes,
Their sons, with envious fingers,
Will gripe each other's throats;

'Or, in more decent fashion,
Will part to meet no more.
But we—no strife or passion
Came ever near our door.

'Yes, we have lived united;
And, wheresoe'er we go,
Our love shall last unblighted,
Through happiness or woe.

'Edwin! take thou my rifle.
That rifle now is thine.
I cannot fairly stifle
The wish it still were mine!

'But shall I grudge it unto
The steadiest hand and eye
In the whole land—my son, too?
No, no!—loved friend, Good-bye.

'Now, Harold!'—sudden pallor
O'erspreads the old man's cheek;
With all his wonted valour
He struggles hard to speak.

But o'er him comes a numbness,
He scarce can draw his breath,
He sinks in fainting dumbness;—
It seems, but is not, death.

They lift his head up slowly:
Their heads with grief are bowed;
They stand in silence holy,
While Silas prays aloud;—

Beseeching God to hearken,
And from his servant's brain
Remove the clouds that darken;
Restore him once again

To consciousness, and lengthen
His hours a farther space,
To supplement and strengthen
Whate'er of Christian grace

Is needful yet deficient :
For though the saintliest,
In view of the Omniscient
Could not abide the test

Of scrutiny, when scanned hard,
Yet, truly, some there be
(As here) below the standard
Of common poverty

In Heavenly riches,—wherefore
(In the blest Saviour's name
They urged the prayer, and therefore
Might gracious answer claim,

With pardon for offences,)
They prayed for him they loved,
That in his perfect senses—
'Stay, stay! He moved—he moved!'

Ianthe spake,—rose regal,
And there rejoicing stood.
Said Silas—'Like the eagle
He hath his strength renewed.'

'Eagles! Who talks of eagles?'
Cries Greenwood: 'round my chair
I hear them yelp like beagles.'
They listen in despair.

The stout old brain was stirring:
But would it e'er come back
From fancies vain and erring,
Into the narrow track

Whereon they fain had led it
To march tow'rds Zion's hill?
Hush!—hark!—he speaks. 'I said it:
Those eagles—eagles—still!

'Why should they make these forays
To screech into my ear?
It's pleasant in the corries,
But devilish down here.'

Oh, who can tell what sadness
Fell on the loving band,
To hear such words of madness!
Ianthe lays her hand,

That soft hand white as cream, on
Her father's throbbing brow,
And partly scares the demon
That chafes his spirit now.

At once more calm and haler,
He smiles; then lightly says:—
'Now who would think, Jock Taylor,
That you 've been all these days

'A grave and reverend stalker?
By this time you might guess
That no one likes a talker
When stags are near him. Yes,

'The wind is fair and steady.
Again that piercing cry!
Thrice it has pealed already—
The eagle 's drawing nigh.

'Hark to his savage screaming!
Those deer are moving fast,
Around the corrie streaming:—
Ah! here he comes at last.

'See how the calves are cowering,
Poor little spotted things!
How grand, how overpowering,
The whistle of his wings!

'O faithful hinds! unyielding
Ye wait his wild career,
Your tender young ones shielding—
What, what is this I hear?

'What?—what?—oh, in the distance—
That scream again!—his mate—
Which means—to his assistance—
Too late—too late—too late!'[26]

* * * *

His breath came short and broken;
Life slowly lost its hold:
His speech was left unspoken,
His tale remained untold.

Some formless words he muttered,
And closed his fading eyes,
One feeble moan he uttered,
Then drooped—as if to rise

No more. But, all amazing,
He raised himself upright,
With eyes wide open, gazing
At some enthralling sight:

Then sudden he upstarted,
And to his feet he sprang;
His lips convulsive parted,
And thus he spake—half sang:—

'My beautiful, my own one, thou comest from above,
And all my heart is yearning sore for comfort of thy love.
The years since we have parted have made thee wondrous fair;
More bloom upon thy lovely face, more sheen upon thy hair,
Than in the sweet and sunny day of tender youthful bliss,
When first thy lips were pressed to mine in one long, loving kiss.
Say, vision bright and gentle, what message dost thou bring?
On thy smooth brow a crown of gold, and on thy hand a ring!
And over me thou wavest a lily in full blow!
Thou comest as a herald, love, to call me from below.

But ah! what mystic regions are now to be explored?
I care not, darling,—thou art here to lead me to the Lord.
I care not: His thou art, love, He will not part with thee;
And nought shall ever part us twain, to all eternity.
And thou wilt guide my spirit far with thine adoring eyes,
And we shall live and love for aye in lovely Paradise.'

He spoke as if transported
With joy, at death's fair charms;
Then sinking, died:—supported
In sweet Ianthe's arms.

Thus through the cloud that gathers
A stream of sunshine flows.
His corpse is with its fathers:
His soul is—where? God knows.

BEN DIXIE.[27]

THERE are times in the life of a man, when he stands
At the point where his pathway divides for the lands
Where the soul after death of the body must dwell,
Either blest in God's home, or unhappy in Hell ;

When a man sees the paths of his destiny plain,
Both the road set for loss and the road set for gain,
Sees the fiends and the angels around him in fight :
I have stood at that point—and, thank God, I chose right.

I 'm the son of a farmer ; a yeoman of worth,
Though he treated his son as he treated the earth,
On an easy old system of shrewd unconcern—
Little labour and outlay, with little return.

But my mother—God bless her !—(how oft to the skies
Such a prayer from the heart for a mother will rise !)
Ever toiled for my good with a measureless love,
Till she left this poor world for the regions above.

I was young when she died; and was known as a lad
Neither active and useful nor idle and bad;
Now and then I indulged in a glass and a song,
And got blamed for not working and pushing along.

But you see I was young, and few people begin
To be earnest in youth about virtue and sin;
I was kindly and merry, and held it no crime
To assist other fellows in wasting their time.

Farmer Dale, our best friend, was a man rather old,
Much beloved by the poor and as honest as gold;
Never rich, he had always enough for his need;
Not a talker or meddler, but godly indeed.

In the schools of affliction his soul had been trained,
Wife and children all gone, save one child that remained;
As a rose was her sweetness, and Rose was her name,
And in loveliness she and the flow'r were the same.

Neither slim in her figure nor grand in her height,
She was graceful and dignified, tender and bright;
And her dark hazel eyes had the gleam and the glow
Of a crisp sunny pool that is quiet below.

She and I were companions for many a day,
In our homes and abroad, in our work and our play;
So we mingled our lives till they seemed but as one,
And our love was complete ere we knew it begun.

But alas! very seldom a mortal need hope
That the pathway of fate will be all on a slope.
This is well—can a heath come to arable use
Till you plough it and work it to make it produce?

So with me. My old father quite suddenly died,
And I stood, scarce of age, without partner or guide;
For good Dale at the time was approaching his end,
And his soul followed hard on the soul of his friend.

Oh! if years had been giv'n him—yes, one year alone—
Till I gathered the rose-bud and made her my own,
It had saved me from bearing a sorrowful blot
Of ill-doings,—repented of, never forgot!

But the past is the past—it has gone to its rest;
Let us work in the present and hope for the best:
From ourselves to ourselves some forbearance is due,
Leaving judgment to Him who alone judges true.

To return to our story. Dale owned, as I 've said,
Little wealth but the toil of his hands and his head ;
And for Rose there remained such a pitiful store,
That she scarcely could pay for the mourning she wore.

At this sorrowful time I was far from the place,
Nor for days knew the worst, though ill news fly apace ;
It was business, not pleasure, that led me to roam,
And I sighed for the hour that would see me at home.

No one sent me the tidings, I heard them indeed
By a chance. Then returning with uttermost speed,
I went straight for Dale's farm :—to the heart I was cut,
For I found the door locked and the shutters all shut.

Yes, the rose of my love had been carried away
By a kind friendly hand. When they let in the day
To the dark silent dwelling, I found on the floor
A sealed note for myself, which had dropt near the door.

'Twas a letter from her : it was meánt for the Post,
But had fallen unmarked by the bearer. At most
We were robbed of the chance of a loving farewell,
For events had run quicker than letters could tell.

On a sudden, Miss Blount—only child of our Squire—
Going Southwards for health, had expressed her desire
That my Rose should attend her with comforting aid,
Half as friend and companion, and half as her maid.

So they hurried abroad, by the Doctor's command,
And were well on their way to a far foreign land:
'They are merry,' thought I, 'while, deserted and lone,
I am left in the cold'—I was angry, I own.

Now it happened just then that some Races were held
At the town where I marketed;—partly impelled
By the pride that inclines you to injure yourself
If you fancy you're slighted and put on the shelf,

And a little by wish for excitement and fun,
I went off to the meeting: the day was not done
Ere I managed to lose all the cash in my purse,
And to gain some bad friends—a misfortune much worse.

Yes, they came and they stayed with me,—called me the
choice
Of good lads,—such a singer, such taste and such voice!
And they taught me to gamble (and plundered me well),
And they led me a dance to the doorway of Hell.

Was I happy? you ask. I felt just as well off
As did he who ate husks with the swine in the trough;
Though a great deal too stubborn to weep and repent,—
And the more sorry-hearted, the lower I went.

I had heard from, and sometimes had written to, Rose,
But (as fire will not mingle with slush, I suppose,)
Correspondence between us lost all of its ease,
And it languished and sickened, and died by degrees.

One fine evening in spring, as I briskly rode back
After market and dinner, there came on my track
Mr. Pue, the old organist,—'Neighbour,' cries he,
'Pray hold hard for a moment, and listen to me!'

'What d'ye think, Master Ben!' he continued, 'Rose Dale
Has arrived with Miss Blount, looking hearty and hale.
Ha, ha, hah! little Cupid 's preparing for sport!
Spin along, my dear fellow, to Blunderby Court!'

As it chanced (nay, *as usual*—'tis sad to narrate)
I was pretty well drunk, something more than elate;
So I rattled my spurs into Challenger's ribs,
And he scattered the mud like a volley of squibs.

When I got near the Court, by a strange kind of luck,
Who should meet me but Rose!—then my liquor-bred pluck
Played me false, and I seemed to have lead in my skull,
And felt awkward and silly and savagely dull.

Oh! I don't care to think of it. Rose very calm,
And as frozenly sweet as an icicled balm;
I, like frost-bitten heaps of fermenting old straw,
A bad mixture of coldness and horrible thaw.

'Come!' said I to myself, 'it's a poor sort of plan
To be scared at fine manners—I'll woo like a man.'
'Come!' said I to sweet Rose—'let's have done with all this!
When shall we two be wed?'—and I gave her a kiss.

She withdrew from my touch, less in anger than pride,
But a tear wet her cheek, and I think that she sighed.
'Never! never!' she answered, 'I'd rather be dead
Than by drunkard be wooed or by drunkard be wed.'

Then I shuddered, and felt as if struck by a dart,
I was sobered at once by the pain at my heart;
And I begged and implored her to pity my case,
And to come to my home as its angel of grace.

Ah! she wept, half-relenting; but Heav'n was her shield—
It was hard to deny me, but ruin to yield—
'Spare! oh spare me!' she said, 'from this sorrowful strife;
Till you grant me one boon I can ne'er be your wife.'

'Well, declare it, my darling!' said I, much inclined
To believe she was yielding through weakness of mind:
Then she points to the sky—'You must solemnly swear,
By your hopes of Salvation, and happiness *there*—

'Thro' that light which the Evil One fain would eclipse,—
That a drop of strong drink shall ne'er enter your lips,
Until first my consent to the act has been given:
You shall make me this vow in the sight of high Heaven.'

How I begged her and prayed her to spare me the vow!
'Only trust me,' said I, 'to be prudent, for now
I desire above all things to turn a new leaf,
And renounce ev'ry habit that causes you grief.

'But the vow—nay, to that I can never consent,—
To be bound by a promise I'd keep, yet repent;
It would vex me so sorely I think I should die—
For I'd ne'er break my promise, no liar am I.'

All in vain my attempts! she stood fast by her word;
Neither tenderness moved her nor bitterness stirred:
Then my love became anger, humility fled;
And I sprang to my saddle, and fiercely I said—

'O you poor-hearted prude! go and find, if you can,
Some old woman to live with you—I am a man.
But as plain honest manhood appears not to suit,
You shall see what I'll be, now you've turned me to brute.'

Then I drove my long spurs into Challenger's sides,
And he rushed like a bull that a tiger bestrides;
And I spurred him and spurred him, till reeking we stopped
At the door of the 'Dragon:'—then off him I dropped,

And away to the Tap-room, with curses, I went,
Yelling oaths that a fiend might rejoice to invent;
Then behaved like a beast—but no beast ever trod
That was vile as a man in rebellion to God.

Oh, the life that began! I was struck with surprise
At the depths I could fall and the heights I could rise:
When you wilfully start on a devilish course
The foul demons possess you and lend you their force.

Such a swine in my sottishness, yet in my mirth
So inspired with a cleverness new in its birth :
Never sated with sin, in the mire I would roll
And exult in my courage in killing a soul.

Half my hours were consumed in debauching and play,
And my earnings grew small and my cash sped away ;
But amidst all the evils one virtue stood fast,—
I was honest ; and thence grew redemption at last.

For, in spite of misconduct, so great was my name
As a judge of good cattle, that orders still came
To view beasts on commission, to buy them or sell ;
And this kept me in bread, also served me right well

By employing my mind ; and the journeys I made
Took me far from the villains whose company laid
Many weights on my soul ;—a detestable crew,
Paltry 'leg,' petty sharper, small usurer Jew.

There was Jessamy Jake, with his ringlets in coils,
An uncleanly old vendor of pictures in oils ;
There was Twopenny Bloat, an unwholesome young lad,
One who traded in ballads offensive and bad.

There was—nay, let me spare you the rest of the lot,
Just another I 'll mention—a wonderful sot—
Joey Peggram, the 'leg;' though more dirty than smart,
(Joey 'Pigworm' by nickname), the man had some heart.

The old Host of the 'Dragon'—delighted to see
Such a set of good topers—quite doated on me;
I had brought him much custom, my songs and my fun
Kept his business alive. He would call me his son;

He would wink when his daughter Matilda appeared—
Very handsome and bold, like a boy without beard,—
'There 's a sight for sore eyes!' he would whisper; 'I say,
Master Bennie, that girl will have something some day!'

It was well understood I had but to propose,
And the girl would be mine any day that I chose;
With a Note for a Thousand the noon we were wed,
And a heap of the same when her father was dead.

A temptation I felt it, yet somehow my mind
Rather shrank from the business, though greatly inclined;
Then my debts grew so pressing, my income outrun,
I determined at last that the thing must be done.

But—as if by some friend for my welfare contrived-
While I thought about yielding, a letter arrived:
'Twas a note from the Squire,—and he bade me set forth,
By the quickest Express, for a place in the North

Where some Shorthorns were kept (of a wonderful breed,
High in fashion), inspect them, then come with all speed
To his Lodge in the Highlands, and give my advice
As to this one and that one—shape, pedigree, price.

So I went to the herd. Much indeed to admire,
And the heifers were lovely as heart could desire,
Such a roan! such a red!—nay, I'm bound to be short—
So behold me at Dola to make my report.

What a glorious glen! I was lost in delight
As I gazed upon mountains so verdantly bright,—
The high slopes, and the summits and clefts of the rocks,
Rich and green as a meadow. Magnificent flocks

Of trim Cheviots—but halt! I am moving too slow.
Dola Lodge was a cottage, long, whitewashed, and low;
With a bench near the door,—there I settled to wait
Till the Squire should come in—he was apt to be late.

So I rested a while. As you well may suppose,
All the tide of my thinking set strongly to Rose.
Is she here? Shall we meet? Will she count me as friend,
Or regard me as foe? If we meet—to what end?

She can never be mine. Could my spirit agree
To be chained by her fancies?—a man must be free!
Then besides,—about cash—what a world of regret
You create for yourself if you marry on debt!

Such a horrible nuisance, too, living by rule,
Doing everything right like a baby at school.
With Matilda one's life would go smoothly along—
We could both be content to do everything wrong—

Nearly everything, say,—yet that cuts it too fine,
'Twould be delicate handiwork drawing the line!
Then my thoughts made a picture of villainous hue:
So I stopped,—raised my head, and looked round at the
view.

There were crags and great mountains, behind and before;
There were rivers that ran with a rush and a roar;
And the green level valley lay peaceful and still,
Dotted over with cattle that wandered at will.

Oh, how pleasant the scene!—it must surely be best
To surrender excitement for innocent rest.
What is wealth—a poor moveable thing like a glove—
To compare with the treasures eternal of love!

'O thou silly milk-hearted one!' something exclaimed
In the depths of my being—'love should not be named
With a psalm-singing chant, and a whine, and a pule:
Master Ben, you 're an idiot, a nincompoop fool.'

Then the voice seemed to tell me of endless delight;
Of all pleasures by day and all pleasures by night;
Of the riches that waited me, heaps upon heaps;
Of the money one earns and the money one keeps:

And it talked about Poverty's dulness and pains;
Of the love that gets cold and the beauty that wanes;
Of the children that come, the expenses that grow;
Of the soul that is sick and the purse that is low:—

And I felt quite distracted. Then fairly I said,
'It is good for a man to be devil, or dead.
For it 's far too perplexing when conscience comes in,
To deride if you lose and torment if you win.'

And I rose from the bench, and I tramped round and round,
Gnashed my teeth, made deep scores with my heel on the
ground;
And the great drops of sweat poured like rain from my
brow,—
And one course now I chose, and the other one now.

But at length came a lull and a deadness of brain;
And I said to myself—'Here is trouble in vain!
Like a leaf that spins free as it sails down the blast,
I decide this or that—Fate determines at last.'

Then I paced up and down; till observing a door
In the wall just in front of the cottage—(grown o'er
With thick ivy and woodbine, and partly o'er-laid
By two larches, where chaffinches fluttered and played,

Partly hid by old laurels)—I lifted the latch;
Lo! a small sheltered garden, most cunning to catch
Ev'ry ray of the sun, yet to baffle the storm;
Very open and airy, though quiet and warm.

There were gooseberries, raspberries, currants, and pease;
There were fuchsias and lilies, and roses like trees;
And a walk, edged with heather more blooming than neat,
Led you down to an arbour,—a rustical seat

Half imbedded in creepers;—this scarce could be seen
For a cairn of white quartzes, which stood like a screen;
Pleasant herbs, mosses, ferns, in its crevices grew,
And its crest was of juniper mingled with yew.

But I cared not to stay in a spot so confined,
So I chose out a resting-place more to my mind,
Near the uppermost wall,—thence I gazed without bar
On the garden before me, the mountains afar.

And the scent of the flow'rs and the balsamy trees,
And the murmurous hum of the busy brown bees,
And the warble of birds and the bleating of sheep—
Ah! the paradise lullaby soothed me to sleep.

And I dreamed a strange dream (which I never will tell),
Of good angels and fiends, of Matilda, of Hell,
Of myself, and of Rose in an agonised prayer:
I awoke, calling Rose,—and behold! she stood there.

Such a glow and a glory around her were shed,
Such a diademed modesty compassed her head,
That I shivered with awe: then as soft as a dove
Flew a smile to her eyes, and I melted with love.

And I fell at her feet, and implored her to save
A poor penitent soul from the Evil One's grave:
'O my Rose! O my darling!' I sighed, 'wilt thou now
Bid me hope for thy love if I yield thee the vow?

'I have lived such a life, that the sight of thy face
Is a boon I deserve not; I mourn my disgrace.
Yet believe me—sweet Rose—though so fallen still true:
Trust me, Rose, only trust, and thou never shalt rue.'

What a radiance celestial illumined her smile!
So angelic in gladness—yet tears all the while
Flowed in womanlike pity: she bent o'er my head,
Laid her hands on my brow, gently kissed it, and said,

'Art thou come to me then, like a bird to the nest,
Sorely wounded and sorrowful, seeking for rest?
Didst thou fear that thy loved one would drive thee away?
—I have loved thee, I love thee, for ever and aye!'

As she uttered these words, o'er the depths of my soul
Seemed a spring-tide of life everlasting to roll:
And I rose up exultant,—Hell's captive restored
To the light of the sun and the light of the Lord.

Even thus was it ended—the conflict was done,
Ev'ry fiend was defeated,—the angels had won;
And the man who was fought for and helped in his need,
All unworthy, was granted a conqueror's meed,

(For high Heav'n is not bound by the measures of Earth,
Nor appraises its gifts by man's pitiful worth),
I was raised from the dust through the bounty Divine,
Then enriched with all good—for Rose Dale became mine.

Oh the blessedness, peacefulness, sweetness of life,
That companion the love of a husband and wife!
They rejoice in the present, the future, the past,—
What are 'chances and changes' to love that will last?

Many years have slipt by, many autumns have fled,
Since my Rose to a home by her husband was led,
Since the bells set their jubilant voices to say,
'They are blended together for ever and aye!'

But the Lord has been constant in blessing, has sent
Sons and daughters to love us and share our content;
He has blessed us with happiness, blessed us with health,
He has blessed us with friendship and honour and wealth.

And the angel who carries all time on his wings,
As he passes and passes us joyfully sings,—
'Still they love and they love, as the day follows day;
They are blended together for ever and aye.'

Oh, how blest is the man that is blessed with a wife
In whose heart there is love, in whose soul there is life!
Let him love her, and trust her to help him to rise
From the mists of the earth to the sheen of the skies.

Yea, for souls thus united in pureness of love,
There is peace in the world, there is glory above;
And whatever befall them united they stay,
They are blended together for ever and aye.

PIGWORM AND DIXIE.[28]

WELL! if ever a man is in want of a wife
To poison his pleasure and pester his life,
First place let him go to Ben Dixie's, you know,
And see what that awful example will show.

Oh, such a good fellow was rollicking Ben,
Beloved by the girls and the right sort of men!
You may call me a lie, but—'pon honour 'tis said—
For a twelvemonth he never went sober to bed.

Yes; rollicking Ben was a fellow of sense,
Who hated all stick-me-up, humbug pretence;
As to that I can swear, for no hogs in the sty
Were more thick with each other than Dixie and I.

What a jolly old crib was his house in the dale,
A Garden of Eden of 'baccy and ale:
Any hour of the day you could eat at your ease,
There were always some ends of cold bacon or cheese.

Lawk! now if you enter his prig of a house,
Not a scrap can you find that would serve for a mouse;
And you wait and you wait till the dinner comes in,
Though perhaps you 're as hungry and thirsty as sin.

But at last there 's a row,—jingle-jing goes a bell,
And you sit yourself down, and you feed like a swell.
Oh, that shiny new tablecloth!—give me the cheer
Of the old one, all gravy and mustard and beer!

Ah yes, Mrs. Dixie, you 're awfully neat,
With your fat little hands and your smart little feet;
And you trot up and down, and you perk up your head,
And you smell like a rose in a lavender bed.

And you smirk and you smile, and you puff out your
breast
Like a pigeon a-pouting and walking its best;
And so mighty polite—why, a fellow can't dare
To chaff when he wants to, and swagger and swear!

Lawk! I 'd like to yell out, like a throttle-choked hen,
When I think of the days of good *bachelor* Ben;
No wife to torment one, dressed up like a doll,—
But that jolly kind creature, young housekeeper Moll.

She was something to see, as you smoked in your chair,
With her rolling black eyes and the kink in her hair;
With her shoes down at heel, and her cheeks pink as paint,
And holes in her stockings—no beastly constraint!

And her ringlets they smelt like a hairdresser's shop:
And her dress was green stuff, spattered over with slop:
And her hands were good large ones, her ankles were thick,
And her nails they were bitten clean down to the quick.

She 'd a taste of a temper, but nothing like vice—
It is downright unchristian to be too precise;
For a shy with a bottle I don't know her match;
But good lawk! what is that when a fellow can catch?

Oh, wasn't it prime! you could drink, you could smoke,
You could chuck out a curse, you could sing, you could joke;
Things are changed now, alas!—all is bother and bore,—
Why, the Missus looks wild if you spit on the floor!

Faugh! to hear how they jaw, it quite gives one a turn,—
As if words were hot mealy potatoes that burn;
'A little more beef, please,'—then faces they pull;
Can't he say,—'Shove us over some more of the bull'?

Yes, I hate the whole set with their finikin ways.
It was 'live and let live' in the jolly old days,
The hens in the kitchen took all that they chose,
And the pups in the parlour rolled over your toes.

But now (set us up!) they 've a precious fine lot
Of young-uns who gobble the pick of the pot;
And they sit up so pert, each small brat in its place,
And when stuffed nigh to bursting they squeak out a grace!

Well, perhaps I 'm not perfect, though fairly so-so;
But, thank Heav'n, I 'm no hypocrite--hang it all, no!
Before I 'd go in for that sanctified bosh—
I 'd as soon send a red flannel shirt to the wash!

Jolly Ben, bless his soul! when he used to begin
He would swear till you thought the old Deuce had come in:
Now see him with Missus, as prim as a pea,
Trudging slowly to church, with the brats in their lee.

Mrs. Dixie got up in her lavender dress;
And poor Ben such a swell as no words can express,
With white pants, and a rose, and a tile with a twist,
And a pair of small girls hanging on to his fist.

So they toddle along to the jole of the bell,
And they go to a pew, and get blest with a spell
Of singing and preaching and things in that style—
Ben sleeps, I 'll be bound, for the most of the while!

But humbug for ever! hypocrisy pays,
Like the bills on the walls about pickles and plays;
Yes, it 's worth heaps of cash to be called 'honest Ben,'
And be toadied and praised by all manner of men.

Who but he! they can't meet to be jolly and dine,
After judging the horses and cattle and swine,
But up starts Squire Blount—'Fill a bumper,' says he,
'For a toast in which no one can fail to agree,—

'The health of that pattern to farmers and all,
Mr. Benjamin Dixie of Rosemary Hall!'
Then they clap their fat paws, and they roar, and they swill—
Euch! bring me a basin, I 'm going to be ill.

If there's one thing I hate it 's that bumptious conceit—
To set up to be tidy and pretty and neat:
It 's as much as to say to a fellow, you see,
'What does nicely for you is not fit for big me!'

Instead of the grass and the puddles of muck,
And the sow with her piggies, and goosey and duck,
And a midden, and plenty old kettles and tubs,
They've got gardens and roses, and things they call shrubs.

Just you walk through the garden and tear off a flow'r
For a shy at the hens--don't the Missus look sour!
Or go near those cantankerous buffers of bees—
After you, sir, is manners; you first, if you please!

Why those brutes won't abide me I really can't say,
For whenever they see me they hunt me away:
They object to bad smells,—but that isn't my case,
Few days but I souse both my hands and my face.

Now Ben Dixie he scrubs in a terrible way,
Till he shines like a sixpence and smells of new hay;
I liked him far better all mire, muck, and grease,
When the man and his midden were quite of a piece.

What nonsense they talk about scrubbing off dirt—
As if things that come natural ever could hurt!
But Ben, the big booby, has grown like the eels,
The more he is skinned, the more lively he feels.

If you stay for the night at that Rosemary Hall,
You 're a mighty queer chap if you like it at all.
'Fresh air,' quoth the blockhead! I say it 's a chouse
To hang out in a windmill and call it a house.

And there 's lots of oak panels as bright as the stars,
And the place stinks of roses and blue-and-white jars;
And your bed 's got white curtains that can't be drawn
round,
And you tumble and grunt like a pig in a pound.

And you 're nearly sent mad with the peppery smell
Of dead flow'rs dry in bowls, and of live ones as well;
And the nightingales sing till you wish 'em in Spain,
And at dawn you 've the thrushes and blackbirds again.

And your nice morning sleep is disturbed by the noise
Of dear Ben's blessêd darlings, his girls and his boys,
A-feeding the turkeys with stuff from a pail,
And screechy pea-devils with eyes in the tail.

And there 's booing of oxen and mooing of cows;
And the hogs and the horses—confound 'em for rows!
And the sheep, and the cur-dog bow-wowing the flock:
Oh, of course! Master Dixie keeps excellent stock.

Poor wretch! I don't fancy that anything pays
For toiling and moiling—I live all *my* days:
A sort of a god, with my 'baccy and bowl,
As jolly and snug as a toad in a hole.

No, it ain't mighty grand, but it suits to a T,
It 's a capital den for a fellow like me.
No draughts and dry roses to keep you a-snort,
But a sensible place looking into a court.

On the ground-floor of course,—I object to a stair,
For the higher you go you get more of the air;
The grate 's pretty big, but the window 's quite small—
Such a fit, sir! in fact it won't open at all.

There ain't neither shutter nor bothersome blind,
But there 's dust on the glass, and the sun keeps behind;
And I snooze on my bed for the most of the day,
And the best of the night I am up and away.

Oh, it 's jolly to lie on your back half a-doze,
And to kick off the quilt with your lazy old toes;
And you stare at your stockings as long as you please,
And you wriggle your trousers right over your knees.

Then you stretch, and get hold of your pipe for a whiff,
And make matters serene with a drop of the "stiff;"
If you 're peckish inclined, there is nothing to do
More easy than fry a red herring or two.

As Bill Shakespeare remarks, 'There is no place like home,'
I 'm as proud of my crib as a cock of his comb;
Life 's sweet there—though once, I must really confess,
I had nearly dropped in for a bit of a mess.

A young cove he came canting with tracts on the sly,
" Converting " he called it: 'Now, Mister,' said I,
' Unless your name 's " Walker " this instant, d' ye see,
We 'll " convert " you to sausage, will Towzer and me.'

So he turned—did this cove—pretty white in the gill:
' Good-day, sir,' says he; ' as you like me so ill,
I 'll never come in to annoy you no more,—
Though I 'm bound to be sometimes a-passing your door.'

Well, before it got dark on that very same day,
I was taken all no-how, a queer kind of way;
All my bones and my gizzards were aching like fun,
And my brains were like boots hanging out in the sun.

Oh, I felt monstrous bad, and I soon got so weak
I could scarce raise my head, and I hardly could speak;
And no creature came near me, I thought I should die,—
When at length sounds the step of a man passing by.

And old Towzer he kicks up a deuce of a din,
And the door opens slow, and a fellow peeps in—
Nick Chousem, my partner;—says he, 'Here 's a go!
Bye-bye, Joey Pigworm,—it 's small-pox, you know.'

And I lay and I blubbered. The rest I forget.
When I opened my peepers, the first thing they met
Was the mission-cove, watching me anxious and fond,
Like a hen whose small ducks are a-swim in a pond.

Well, of course I recovered—that 's middling clear,
For if I 'd skedaddled I shouldn't be here:
That good cove pulled me out of Old Gooseberry's gripe,—
And his tracts came quite useful for lighting one's pipe.

Not ungrateful, sir, no! he declined my advice,
But I showed him neat things with the cards and the dice;
And my dog runs to meet him a-wagging its tail,
And it grins 'How d' ye do ' like a shark in a gale.

No, it don't pay a bit to be seedy, you see,—
Not, at least, for mere common-sense snobbies like me:
But Ben!—let his thumb ache, they rush to inquire,—
Town, village, and country, lord, parson, and squire.

Lawk, when Ben comes to die! bless their heads and their eyes,
How the crape and the white pocket-wipers will rise!
And the funeral cards will be scattered like peas,
And the folk will come swarming like mites on a cheese.

And they 'll drive up a gimcracky hypocrite hearse;
And they 'll shove him inside, like a pig in a purse;
And they 'll carry him off to the burial crib;
And the parson will come, like a rook in a bib.

Then they 'll earth up his corpse in a daisy-bank hole;
And the boom of the organ will sweep off his soul,
As you blow off the froth from a buzzy brown bowl:
And the bloodhound bell will jole—jole—jole.

O lawk! can't I see it? And afterwards too,
The Missus and children all making boohoo;
And creeping like blackbirds down Sweetbriar Lane,
A-weeping, and wishing him with them again

And the little pale girls in their bombazine stuff,
With their hair running loose like a parcel of fluff,
And nice flow'rs in their hands for the grave of "Papa"--
Such a comfort to Ben in his coffin, ha ha!

Rum business is life! but it ends all apiece
For the easy good chaps and the hard-working geese:
And why should they grudge a poor beast of a man
To be happy and jolly the best way he can?

Says the mission-cove once,—'You 've no sort of excuse
For to cumber the earth, if you 're no sort of use.'
'How,' says I, 'could the beggarsome planet be filled,
If the coves that do nothing were taken and killed?'

Some fine day, by and by, I shall likely expire—
They 'll not take up Joe Pigworm in char'ots of fire;—
Well! when Gooseberry wants me I 'll meet him quite brave:
I wonder what folk will strew over *my* grave!

Nick Chousem, I daresay, will miss me a bit,
And he 'll sit on my grave, and he 'll smoke there and spit;
And perhaps I 'll be missed by my brute of a dog,
For I lick him and kick him, and give him his prog.

Lawk, what do I care! My blest body will rot,
My blest soul (if I 've got one) will toddle to pot,
And I 'll treat the poor worms to a famous repast—
Oh yes, I 'll be useful to something at last!

THE ANCHORITE.[29]

THE anchorite was tall and grim,
And long of hair and long of limb,
And mighty of chest, and lank and slim;
His eyes were mad and wide and wild,
And deathly sad and ghastly mild.

He raised his face and long lean jaw,
And gaped his mouth like lion's maw,
And sent up a shriek that seemed to draw
All hope and comfort from the air—
A shriek of nethermost despair.

He cursed the Moon:—Thou asterisk!
Thou pestilent putrescent disc!
Thou eyed with the eye of the basilisk!
Thou smiling harpy-hearted queen,
Blight blast thee and thy baneful sheen!

'Twas thus thou smiled that noxious night—
So modest-mild, so meek and bright—
Thou cockatrice-eye! thou hypocrite!
When naked Fulvia frantic stood,
And soaked the sand with sacred blood.[29]

Ah, Fulvia, of the yellow hair,
Ah, Fulvia, more than Venus fair,—
How passionate strange the look you wear,
As all alone our way we take
Through wood and wold and willow-brake!

Through wood and wold and o'er the hill
You lead me at your utter will,
With mystical chants that madly thrill;
Through rugged rifts our way we make,
Until at last we reach the lake.

There, on a rock whose mass divides
The current of the shore-set tides,
Cold glimmers a tripod's golden sides;
And, stone-like still, upon the sands
A tender little maiden stands.

And then—beneath yon modest Moon—
You light your fires, and waken soon
Mad magical fumes: I tremble,—swoon,—
You touch my lips with Samian wine,—
I wake—I see you all divine!

Beside the tripod's gleaming gold
My love-inebriate eyes behold
Your naked body's majestic mould—
O ivory-mellow miracle!
What waves of beauty sink and swell!

Near, near you come, and yet more near,
You whisper magic in my ear,
I tremble—unmanned by sudden fear;
You seize the maid, and bare her breasts,
Which throb like dovelets in their nests.

—You took the steely adder-tongue
That from your jewelled cestus hung,
And buried it deep; and then you flung
The dying maiden on the shore,
And scanned the marks her fingers tore![29]

Then ghastly terror o'er me spread,
Hot flames of horror racked my head.
Away—far away—I fled, I fled;
And tempests howled, and torrents poured,
And Heaven's tremendous thunder roared.

I ran—I ran—through fire and flood;
The magic poison in my blood
Was working with might. I reach the wood,
But there, beneath a grizzled tree,
I fail, I sink. Then lo! I see

A small and distant flickering shine.
With hope renewed, I take the line
That leads me thither: a ruined shrine—
Wall, pediment, column, architrave,
Heaped in one mass;—it screens a cave,

A deep and dismal rocky rift.
Soft to the place I steal, and lift
Thick ferns asunder; and, through the drift,
Illumined by one feeble light,
I look upon a solemn sight.

Two men; a mother, babe at breast;
Two children; all so scantly drest
That my pitying eye is forced to rest
On the bared flesh of each lean form
That trembles in the bitter storm.

They crouch around a sculptured stone,
A column's abacus o'erthrown.
The famishing infant makes its moan,
The mother's face is wan and sad:
Yet at that moment all seem glad.

For there, before them, stands the sign
Of Him they worship as divine,—
A fragment of bread, a cup with wine;
And as their lips the symbols press,
They smile with holy happiness.

Then, then indeed, my wondering eyes
At length began to recognise
In these, so uncouth and mean of guise,
Lorn exiles from as great a home
As swelled the majesty of Rome.

Such grievous memories o'er me crowd,
I weep and sob, and sigh aloud:
To see Valeria—once so proud—
Half-naked in the miry clay,
A sheepskin for her whole array!

And Tullius Verus, he whose might,
In many a long and dubious fight,
Had forced the Barbaric hordes to flight;
And blind Herminius, weird of face,
Patrician of a priestly race;

And those twin tender maiden flowers,
That grew so sweet in pleasant bowers,—
Now withered and faded. Lo, the powers
Of Light and Darkness fought amain,
And rent the prey they strove to gain.

Yet nought could shake their holy calm—
Those whom the Christ had fed with balm—
Heav'n smiles from their eyes. They sing a psalm;
Then, with soft tears that soon will cease,
Each gives to each the kiss of Peace.

With heart resolved, I left my place
And went to them, and asked their grace
To succour me in my wretched case;
Sick soul and fevered body call
For liberty from Fulvia's thrall.

In sudden fear they start to flee,
Expectant of an enemy:
I cast myself down on bended knee—
'Receive me, help me,' I exclaim;
'I ask it in your Jesu's name.'

And then they suffered me to stay,
They chased my misery away,
For shades of the night they brought me day;
And from that time somewhile I stood
A member of their Brotherhood.

At length the fiends more fierce arose
And fell upon their Christian foes;
The hunters' strong toils around them close,
And, tracked o'er woodland, hill, and heath,
God's saints are seized and borne to death.

And I—what fate befell me then?
Returned unto the haunts of men,
I revelled in luxury again:
The past unknown, all joys I share,
And sun myself in Fulvia's snare.

And now high festival is held,
To celebrate a nation quelled—
Against the great Empire's rule rebelled,—
Her noblest warriors doomed to die
To glad the sovereign people's eye.

Reclined on cushions soft and broad,
Behold the Emperor—his nod
More terrible than the bolts of God!
I see the emerald in his hand,
As close beside the throne I stand.[29]

And near me lovely Fulvia warms
My heart with love; her fair soft arms,
And her bare beautiful bosom's charms,
On my enraptured senses press
Elysian dreams of perfectness.

The trumpets roar and rave with pride;
The brazen portals open wide;
Then enter the swordsmen, vulture-eyed,
And with them march in sullen show
The victims doomed to suffer woe.

See, first advance with measured tread
The captive warriors—on each head
A helmet, in each right hand a blade;
Mock armature! poor panoply!
Some win, some lose, but all must die.

And close behind them crawl along
A weary ragged Christian throng—
Forced in at the spear's point, scourged with thong,—
Men, women, children, on their way
To be devoured by beasts of prey.

Soon the fierce work of death began.
The swordsmen, slaughtering in the van,
Toiled merciless; blood in rivers ran:
Meanwhile the Christians scatheless stayed,
And smiled and sang, or wept and prayed.

Undaunted, Tullius waited near
His fainting wife—past hope of cheer,
Enthralled, overwhelmed, aghast with fear:
Behind the pillared canopy
I shunned the censure of his eye.

And now arises savage din.
With growls and groans come trooping in
Fell monsters of every clime and kin:
They strive awhile in furious fight,
Before the Christians meet their sight.

Soon they espy their helpless prey,—
They rend and raven, maim and slay.
But calm in the midst of that dread fray
Stands Tullius, grasping in his hand
An axe, uplifted from the sand.

Before Valeria strong he stood,
And long defied the savage brood.
But lo! a lean lioness, grimed with blood,
Breaks through the backward-beaten ring
Of daunted brutes, and stoops to spring.

I mark Valeria's starting eye,
Her gaze of ghastly agony—
Swift, like to the flames that scorch the sky,
Flies the keen axe with fiery stress
And cleaves the crouching lioness!

Then Tullius, all sublime with love,
Raised his wan wife, and onward strove
To the altar of Latialian Jove;
And there, supported in his arms,
He held her safe from instant harms.

Throughout the crowd a murmur ran—
Half rage, half favour for the man
So noble of deed,—keen strife began
'Twixt those who fain would change his fate,
And those immoveable in hate.

The Emperor smiles a cruel smile,
Insidious thoughts his mind beguile;
He turns him around, with eyes of wile
He gazes here and gazes there
On those beside his marble chair.

His searching glances fall on me:
He marks my anxious agony.
'Ha ha! be it thine to speak,' saith he,—
'To save or slay. Doom! haste thee—doom!
The upward, or the downward, thumb?'[29]

I read what scarce he sought to hide.
Perdition gaped on either side:
Black hells of remorse if Tullius died;
But if, through me, he met with grace,
Among the lions were my place.

And as I writhe in wild despair,
Fair Fulvia wreathes her yellow hair,
And dazzles me with the trancing glare
Of eyes that lurid lustre breed—
Woe! woe!—I know not what I did!

* * * * *

An eremit! an eremit!
O life of lives—so sweet, so sweet!
So fitted for me, and I for it!—
Fair larvæ sometimes near me dwell,
And ivory billows sink and swell!

And sometimes Tullius, from the grave,
With pale Valeria, comes to rave:
I chase the cold shadows from my cave,
And, with a yell that shakes the stone,
I scare them back to Acheron.

And when deceitful Luna shines,
I dash my head against the pines,
Or mangle my limbs in the old lead-mines:
But when King Sol is beaming bright,
I am a blessêd anchorite.

An anchorite! an anchorite!
O life of lives—when Sol is bright!
Or Luna is hid from the quiet night!
For then, away my sorrows roll,
And Holy Heaven is in my soul.

THE CHAMORRA.[30]

AMONG the hills of Portugal,
Whose waters hasten from their caves,
As at some proud enchanter's call,
To join the Minho's sweep and fall
Impatient for the Western wave,—

Among these hills of sunny glow
A farm is pleasantly confined,
Its terraced slopes in verdure blow,
With emerald maize bedecked below,
With oaks above and chestnuts twined.

And where the loveliest charms adorn
This glory of the wilderness,
A joyous home confronts the morn,—
Yet laughs the noontide heats to scorn,
So close around it the embrace

Of the broad-foliaged fragrant vine
That all encompasses with shade;
O'er the low roof its tendrils twine,
And o'er the court, by breath of kine
Yet more divinely odorous made.

'Neath the vine-canopy, at rest,
A traveller worn and weary lay,
By toilsome journeying distrest, —
The hospitable farmer's guest
One evening of a summer day.

Their simple feasting done, they share
In friendly talk, the cup goes round,
Brimmed with green wine of virtue rare, —
For, like a docile courser, there
Both force and gentleness are found.[30]

And as their spirits feel the heat
Shed by these subtly genial fires,
In confidence more free they meet,
And each with answer hastes to greet
The curious thought that each inspires.

'Now pardon me,' the farmer cries,
'Your Excellency jesting seems!
That land of yours that distant lies
Beyond the ocean and the skies,
Must be like countries seen in dreams.'

'No lands,' the other says, 'but boast
Some charms or marvels of their own.
Come tell me this, my honoured host,
If thou, so wondering at most
Of the new pictures I have shown,—

'Strange, but yet far from marvellous
To dwellers from their earliest day
'Neath skies more dark and tyrannous,
More frigid and more vaporous,
Than this fair azure,—tell me, pray,

'Hast thou no marvel to impart,
Of higher mystery than those
Concerning harrow, plough, and cart,
And husbandry and city mart,
And how the moony olive grows?

'Hast thou no tale to fright the ears
With sound of ghastly fantasy;
Some tale begot in olden years,
Of witch and wizard, full of fears
Provoked by deeds of devilry;

'Some story fraught with fiendish thrill
To curdle in the veins of man?'
'Yea,' said the farmer, 'have thy will:
A tale I'll tell thee, with such skill
As one of simple nurture can.

'And think not that I dare to use
A lying tongue: I'll tell thee truth.
Let these who hear me straight accuse,
If in the smallest word I choose
To falsify. 'Twas in my youth

'The deeds were done, the sights were seen,
Which 'tis my business to relate;
And though from memory's field I glean,
Such things no lapse of years between
From memory can obliterate.

'I, I that speak, myself I felt
The evils that I now bewail;
For with those hapless ones I dwelt,
On whom the Demon's hatred dealt
Such blows. But hearken to my tale.'

'Mid the Estrica's mountain-billows,
Where many a cow and bleating lamb
Rejoice a farm, that restful pillows
In greenery of sheltered willows,
Near to the town of Cabrasam,—

Within that sunny mountain home
I lived in pleasant servitude;
With the fair flock I oft would roam,
Or guide the ox-plough through the loam,—
Obedient to a master good:

In all ways good: of virtue sure,
That knew no churlish envious taints;
Most generous to the Church and Poor;
A man who seemed to live secure,
Protected by the Holy Saints.

He spent his days in happiness,
Enriched with all that gilds a life;
And blest with that which most can bless,
Of all that mortals may possess,—
A loving and belovêd wife.

Seven months had hurried to a close
Since wedlock made their lives complete;
And now the fragrant fruitful rose
By genial indication shows
The coming of a scion sweet.

No more her household work she plies,
As eager as the early morn;
With lingering step and wistful eyes,
She moves sedate or languid lies,
And muses listlessly forlorn.

Her tender husband strove in vain
To soothe her fanciful distress;
Then lovingly he thought to gain
Good help to save her from the pain
Of self-reproach for idleness;

And so, to bring her cheerful aid,
He searched the country up and down,
For some bright, honest servant-maid;
While on myself command was laid
To seek one in our neighbouring town.

One morn, ere earliest vapours breaking
Revealed the glories of the day,
Behold me on my journey, making
Pontê de Lima nearer, waking
The echoes with a joyous lay.

The road led through a valley small,
Whose crags enclosed a furious river:
Passing around a rocky wall,
Near to a shadowed waterfall,
I saw a sight that made me quiver!

Lonely and sad in the depths of the dell,
Where the wild waterfall, bounding to hell,
Poured out its wrath with a thunderous might,
There rested a woman,—close mantled in brown,
Mobled and muffled from sandal to crown,
Earthy-brown blood-colour,—fronting the light

Wan o'er her face a pale sunbeam was creeping,
Closed were her eyelids, as though she were sleeping,
Yet in her restfulness seemed she to wake.
Through the wide folds of her russety raiment—
Muddy and way-worn, with many a frayment
Shredded and rent in the thorn-bearing brake—

Through the brown raiment her hands were displayed,
Spread to the sunbeam that slid through the shade,—
Hands that were slender and bony and white—
White as the snow,—and they pendulous hung,
Moved to the beat of her pulses, and swung,
Basking like snakes in the chilly-warm light.
Struck with amazement, and sore dismayed,
Back from her nearness myself I flung,
And prayed to the Saints in a sickly fright.

She opened her eyes and fixed them on me
With a blinking stare that was strange to see:
Brown were her eyes—or gray—or green,—
Narrow and long,—and they took the tints
Of the lights that wander in luminous flints,
Rainbow dull-patterned in hyaline,—

And aslant they went o'er her milk-white cheek.
She moved her mantle. Her hair was sleek,
And silvery fulvous flecked with brown ;
'Twas short as the slippery fur of the mole,
That clutches his prey in the darksome hole,
And soft it seemed as the sea-bird's down.

Oh ! she bewitched me : I lost my fears
As I gazed on her beauty. Her delicate ears
Were long and limber, as if to seize
The faint little breath of a coming sound
That speaks of a wild thing's distant bound
In secret places among the trees.

Red were her lips, for the blood within
Bloomed through the half-transparent skin.
She opened her mouth with a stealthy smile,—
And I saw that her teeth were white as the day,
As they gleamed in the sun like a bright array
Of preening swans on a jasper isle.
She fixed my eyes, and they could not stray ;
I could not tear myself away,
Although my spirit foreboded guile.

She smiled again ; then low she said,
'Santinho! are your wits undone,
Because you see me, nearly dead
From cold, with both my hands outspread
To warm them in the morning sun?'

Her voice was blandishing of sound,
Yet something grated in its tone.
I answered—'Much more warmth is found
By walking briskly, I'll be bound,
Than sitting in the wind alone!'

'What if I'm tired, as well as cold?'
The tone was bitter. Then said I,
'Have you all night been walking?' Bold
Said she, 'I have—that's quickly told,—
And many a long night previously.

'A long, long journey I have come,
From Beira's desert mountain sides;
Tarouca is my native home.'
'Why choose,' said I, 'so far to roam?—
But there perhaps a secret hides?'

'No secret, Senhor, sin nor shame,—
I neither mean nor fly from harm;
Joana is my Christian name;
To find employment all my aim,
As servant at some quiet farm.'

She smiled with such simplicity
That all my doubts were swept away,
And in her face I seemed to see
The loveliness of creatures free
That in the pleasant woodlands play.

And through me thrilled a happiness
Commingled with a touch of awe;
As one might feel, who in distress
Beheld a being come to bless—
An angel-presence near him saw.

Lauding the Saints, who thus had cared
To help me in my dubious quest,
I to Joana straight declared
My mission,—and all reckless dared
To seek her for our household guest.

She thanked me with a winning grace,
According me a fair consent,—
And pleasure smiled upon her face.
So to my master's dwelling-place
The maid and I together went.

She sat her down outside the door,
While to my master I related—
And to my mistress (told before
Of all his scheme)—the chance that bore
So fair an aspect. They debated

About the stranger. 'None could scan
Her conduct,—haply she had erred ;'
The cautious farmer thus began :
The wife (whose thoughts more nimbly ran),
Delighted at the tale she heard,

Vowed that the girl from Heaven had dropt ;
For one so young and fair of face
To be "Chamorra"—closely cropt--
Avouched her of an honest race,
(Best workers such, the proverb says).
'Twas fixed : the stranger maiden stopt,
And in the household took her place.[30]

Bright was the hour when the baby was born!
Merriment greeted the news of the morn:
Ne'er such an infant had gladdened the earth;
Welcome him into existence with mirth!
Healthy and hearty, and happy of mien,
Nestled in white as a rose-bud in green!
In come the neighbours with curtsies and bows,
Leaving their poultry, their calves, and their cows;
Thronging, with longing the baby to view,
Craving for ever to see what is new;
Full of warm-heartedness (flimsy as breath),
Brisk at a birth, and demure at a death.

She comes! she comes!
She twirls her thumbs!
She of all Wisdom!—mark her ways,
As on the child she sets her gaze!
Note her steely lucid eye,
Cold as winter in the sky;
See her bony eagle's-beak;
See her ashen-sallow cheek;
See her figure tall and stout,
Muscular yet round-about.
Mark the pursing of her lips!
Note her busy finger-tips—

Decked with nails so fair and neat,
Smooth and rosy, all complete !
From them (with a fitful spark,
Seen by certain in the dark,)
Streams of energy would drain,
Airier than the spray of rain—
Streams of blessing or of bane.

Full on the babe she fixed her eye,
Then, crossing herself, she uttered a sigh ;
'The babe 's bewitched,'—she said.
Loud laughed the father, hearty and high :
Low laughed the mother,—her sole reply—
Too proud to feel afraid.

'Laugh and be merry, good folks all !'
The Wise One muttered ; 'this infant small,
Unless I strangely err,
Is marked by the Devil, as one of the lot
Foredoomed from the womb to bear a blot
Of omen sinister.'

She took up the babe, and its shoulder bared,
And she talked to herself, and stared and glared ;
While, manifest to view,

There shone on the shoulder, so white and warm,
A punctured brand of a crescent form
 And clear sanguineous hue.

'The Devil—the Devil—his mark,' she said,
And crossed herself thrice, and nodded her head.
 We trembled with affright.
'Fear not,' the Wise One whispered, and smiled,
'Nothing can harm the innocent child
 And glut the Devil's spite,
Save when each moon is new in the sky;
Then watch ye the babe with a heedful eye,
 And watch him all the night.'

She crossed herself thrice, and thrice she bent,
Muttering prayers,—and away she went,
 Nor paused to say farewell.
But nigh to the threshold a glance she cast
On a mantled figure, and as she passed
 Spake to it,—'Prithee tell,
O crouching creature muffled in brown,
Wherefore so still art thou cradled down?
 Thou seem'st to slumber well!'
Joana ('twas she) no answer made,
But stirless lay in the mantle's shade,
 As if entranced by spell.

The Wise One chose no longer stay,
But speeded forth on her lonely way.

Month followed month in quiet course:
Our household mill went rolling round,--
Which, like the patient toilsome horse,
We servants moved with steady force,
And life's plain victual simply ground.

'Tis well when in a home prevail
The harmonies by love begun;
When no discordant fiends assail,
And break the bonds that ne'er should fail
To link its inmates into one:

Thus seemed our dwelling; master, men,
Maids, mistress, all alike rejoice:
But human home, or creature's den,
Will ever hold some denizen
With ugly discords in its voice.

And, as when storm-gusts on a lake
Show that wild tempests lurking brood,
So would Joana's anger wake,

And with capricious fervour break
The mildness of her wonted mood.

Ah, what a fury in her eyes!
Their narrow lengths would gleam and glow,
Like pits where lava burning lies
And flame of swift destruction flies
To lay the hapless gazer low.

Her brow would writhe, her lip would curl,
While her keen teeth she gnashed and ground,—
Long shapely teeth more white than pearl;
Her arms she 'd whirl, her frame would furl
As if to make a deadly bound.

But with a shiver she would stay
The strong convulsions of her hate,
And calm her glances glittering-gray;
Then, with still words, that seemed to flay,
To scarify, to lacerate,

Would blight her foe with bitter mock;
Yet, while amazed and terrified
We pressed together—as the flock
Scared by a wolf will closely lock,—
A smile would o'er her features glide,

And all of her would gaily gleam
In coaxingly caressing guise,
And her lithe limber movements seem
To bring before one in a dream
A greyhound's graceful witcheries.

Oh, she was passing fair and sweet!
But—praisêd be the Saints above!—
My heart went never forth to greet
Her heart with tenderness,—unmeet
That maiden for a homely love.
No Paradise, howe'er complete,
Blooms blessedly, for minds discreet,
Where scorpions nestle with the dove.

Although such fiercely-glowing fire
Would rush from her in fitful blaze,
Her general mood might well inspire
Unmingled trust: her plain attire,
Her silentness and modest ways,

Her steady, ceaseless industry,
Without display, without pretence,—
So grave, and yet so fair to see!—
Her mistress won to love, and she
Soon gave her all her confidence.

And thus one day it came to pass,
While talk their needlework beguiled,
The mistress wept, and said, 'Alas,
Joana! would that prayer or Mass
Could aid my little darling child!'

Then she related, word for word,
The Wise One's prophecy of wrong
Designed for babes by Satan blurred:
Silent and still Joana heard,—
Then gently said, 'I 've known it long.

'Long have I known it, yet feared to speak,
Lest from the tints of thy delicate cheek
Terror and sorrow should chase the bloom.
Now will I tell thee tidings of gloom,—
Secrets terrible, secrets dread,
Secrets won from the lips of the dead.

'Know'st thou the bounds of the Devil's power?
Nay, who knoweth!—from hour to hour
Saints and Demons wrestle and fight—
Uppermost lowermost, light or night.
Sometimes the Saints are sore beset,
And Satan seizes the chance to get,

To get and to keep, a masterful hold
O'er the feeble flocks in the Church's fold.
Long, long ago, when the Church, may-be,
Had lapsed for a while from her piety,
And robbed the Saints of their needful share
Of help in the battle through Mass and prayer,
'Twas then that the Devil came forth in might
And won for himself this fearful right:—

'Whenever a babe in Portugal
Slips into the world when the star-beams fall
Mingled and blended and marred in a maze
Of mystical opposites, all ablaze
In a baleful sheen, on the nights of days
Not to be named by a mortal's tongue;
Then, on that luckless babe is flung
A doom removeless by Mass or prayer,
A doom that eludes all watching and care.
The hungry Devil, with hell in his hand,
Comes to the babe and fixes a brand,—
A brand that is full and ruby red
As the swelling buds of the rose's bed,
A brand that is clear and crescentine
As the nightly orb of the silver shine.
Know'st thou what meaneth that blazing brand,
Stamped by the Devil, with hell in his hand?

'When years sixteen have flitted and flown,
The Devil will come to claim his own;
To claim for himself, for the deeds of the dark,
The mortal that beareth the crescentine mark.
Ah! then the youth will sicken and pine,
And feel a strange might in the mystical sign,—
Longing and yearning and anguish within,
The pangs of the serpent that changeth his skin.
And then will he hide in the forest alone,
And writhe on the rocks, and whimper and moan;
And ravenous beasts will list to the sound,
Will gather around him—around—around,—
Wild-cats, as still as the soft-feathered owls,—
Wolves, with low whining and blandishing howls,—
Everything cruel that wanders and prowls.
Around him they go—around!—around!—
With a measured glide and a rhythmical bound;
They coax with the voice and caress with the tongue,—
Till his brain grows sick and his heart unstrung.
And he longs to escape from his man-like form,
And to rush thro' the woods on the path of the storm;
To rend and mangle, to raven and prey,
Where blood is streaming,—away! away!

'Then round him they troop—around—around,—
He howls to the stars, he falls on the ground;

'Twixt living and dying he writhes and burns:
And thus from a man to a wolf he turns,—
A wolf more fell than the forest brood,
For he craves unceasing for human blood.
And whenever he feasts on a victim's corse
The Devil rejoices, and gives him force
To quit the form of the wolfish plan,
And walk for a while in the form of a man.
For years he ravens: at length expires
His term on earth: then Hell and its fires.'

'O babe!' said the mother, and wept and sighed,
'Would that thy life in the womb had died!
Would that thou never hadst breathed and smiled,
Thou wretched—wretched—thrice-wretched child!
Accurst be the fiend-lighted ominous sun
That shone on the world when thy life was begun!
Save him!' she cried in accents wild,
'Mother of Paradise! Mother mild!—
Can nothing be done?—can nothing be done?'

'Hush thee! sweet mistress,' Joana said,
And tenderly raised the mourner's head,
'The remedy is nigh,—
The secret won from the lips of the dead,
In the cavernous pit where the dragons tread:—
Oh cease to weep and sigh!

'When first on the sabled-blue of night
The moon shall rise in her mantle bright
After the midmost hour has tolled,
Bear thou the babe to the mountain height,
And lay him naked to front the light,
Stretched on a blanket wide outrolled.

'Then take thou a dove, and with stroke of a knife
Sever its neck, and with blood of its life
  Anoint the Devil's brand—
On the child it blows like a mystical rose—
Pour on it streams of the blood that flows,
  Nor seek to stint thy hand.

'Leave then thy little one—speedy and soon
Under the eye of the cold white moon
  (Unwatched—or ne'er unslaved!),
And the moon she will suck up the brand thro' the blood,
As she sucks up the sea in the tide of its flood:
  Thus shall thy child be saved.'

Three nights and days elapsing bring
The time to quell the Demon's power;
When the new moon to life did spring,
And freshly-kindled glimmerings fling
O'er the dark earth at midnight's hour.

The infant on the ground is laid,
The crescent brand with blood is sown,
Full many a vow and prayer is made;
Then, shivering in the mountain shade,
We leave the naked babe alone.

Oppressed with anxious thought we turned,
And slowly paced the homeward track;
But the fond father fain had spurned
Ali counsel, for his spirit yearned
With love,—and glad had he gone back

To guard the little one from bane,
Though all the rite were nullified:
Arrived at home, we scarce could gain
Fair promise from him to abstain
From speeding to his infant's side;
This much at length he yields with pain,—
A bow-shot off he will remain,
Nor move unless some ill betide.

With trembling hand he reached, and took
His grandsire's trusty bell-mouthed gun
From off its customary hook,
And down its barrel poured and shook

Six rusty nails.—This scarce was done,
When through the murmurs of the brook
Come shriek on shriek! Aghast we look
Out on the night,—then madly run.

Rolling and falling o'er boulder and block
Onward we rush like the avalanche rock,
Leaping and springing through uttermost glooms;
Shrill on the wind comes the shrieking and screaming,
Mingled with sounds of a devilish seeming—
Laughter of things that grow ruddy in tombs.

Lo the moon rises! her radiance is falling
Cold on the child that is crying and calling;
Grinning and gaping beside him there smiled
Blood-dripping fangs of a hell-wolf, enjoying
Draughts of delightfulness, rending, destroying,
Drinking the life of the innocent child.

'Hell for thee, Devil!' The monster upraising
Eyes that were furnaces glowing and blazing,
Glared at us weirdly. Then, swift as the light,
Sudden with thunder the echoes are ringing!
Bane-bearing missiles are sighing and singing,
Hurled through the air on the message of blight.

Bolts of the blessèd! Heaven's angels were guiding;
Straight to the fiend, ere it crept to its hiding,
All the rough arrows of vengeance were sped;
Prone it fell writhing and twisting and twining,
Speedy I rushed to it,—yearning and pining
But for one stroke ere it sank to the dead.

Down on its shoulder my bludgeon went swinging:
Curses! the Demon escaped from me, springing
Swift from the earth. Then in anguish intense
Howling it crawled, with the shoulder all shattered,
By my strong bludgeon-blow shivered and battered,
Into the forest,—where darkness was dense.

Ah! who shall tell the mother's woe!
Voiceless she wept, no tears she shed,
But like a broken branch lay low,
And all her life appeared to go
To find her infant that was dead.

The sorrowing husband vainly sought
For aid from one required to aid,—
Joana,—vanished!—now a thought
Most fearful to the mind was brought

Concerning her—that stranger maid,—
That she indeed had foully wrought
As those who with the Devil trade.

And as, low-whispering, we conversed,
Each told of her some deed unknown;
Each to the other now rehearsed
Some malice of that fiend accursed,
Who glamour over us had thrown.

Yes, the fair Being sent by fate
In our glad trustful home to dwell,
A monster was—a thing of hate,
That Holy Ones abominate—
Than savage brutes more fierce and fell,—
A "lobis-homem" devil's-mate,
A demon doomed to endless Hell![30]

In the gray of the morn, ere the motherly East
From his slumberous chamber the sun had released,
We sought the lone forest, the sorrowful place
Of dread and disaster: then anxious we trace
The steps of the sore-smitten wolf. Lo! behold!
Bedabbled with blood, and bestiffened with cold,

Scarce a rood from the spot with the slaughter-stains rife,
Joanà lies ghastly, outbreathing her life.
She reads in our eyes the hunger to slay,
Yet fawningly tries to charm it away.
For pity she pleads with her agonised eyes,
Then murmurs in tones that scarce audibly rise—
'At last ye have come! For the whole of the night
I have lain all alone in this terrible plight.
In the strength of a love that o'erpowered my alarm
By the child was I watching, lest shadow of harm
Should fall on his fairness. And when from the wood
Outrushed the wild wolf, by the infant I stood;
I grappled the wolf,—then a thunder-flash leapt,
And I fell to the earth,—then in terror I crept
Through the black-shadowed bushes,—then fainting I fell.
Ah, help me, dear friends! who have loved you so well!'
Most piteous she looked in her pain and affright,
Slim, phantom-like beautiful, snowily white:
Our manhood forbade us to fall on and slay
A creature so feeble;—but, turning away,
In silence we waited, while one of us sped
To bring help from a priest ere her spirit was fled.

Silent we waited; no sound awoke
The still of the woods, save the muffled choke
Of the wan Chamorra's gasping moan,—

And now and again the mellow cries
Of the hoopoe's note, and the clear replies
From bell-voiced reptiles upward thrown ;
　　And past us flitted the butterflies
　　Fair as enamelled evening skies,
　　And golden lizards greenly shone.

For rays of the day they pierced the leaves,
Fell on the earth, and, as one that weaves,
Spun from the moss a weft of haze ;
And burly young warmth came dancing on,—
Like a frolicsome lion—that roars anon,
And fierce in wanton vigour slays.

Sudden, a thrill of a creeping chill
Ran through our veins in trickling rill :
　Perforce we bent our look
Full on a figure that tow'rds us stalked—
The Wise One !—leaning, as she walked,
　On her long hazel crook.

Straight to us came she,—nodded her head,
Stared in our eyes,—and then she said,
'Praised be the Saints !—why rest ye here ?'

'Praised be they ever and ever!'—said we;
'Twelve paces off—beneath yon tree—
There lies a wolf that slew a deer.'
'A wolf indeed it well may be,'
The Wise One said, 'for floating free,
Foul blood-scents taint the atmosphere.'

Twelve paces she walked,—and then she saw
The wretch that lay with upward gaze.
Ah! by the drop of the stiffened jaw,
And the stare of the eyes in their open awe
Half-mocked with a smile on the greeny glaze,
'Twas clear that man and his mortal law
No hand of vengeance now could raise.

'Gone to the fiends!' the Wise One muttered,—
'Tell me the tale!' Then, quickly uttered,
The truth before her all was spread.
Said she—'Whoever could well espy
That narrow and long and murderous eye,
Wolf-nature might at once have read.'

Then from the body away she tore
The orange kerchief its shoulders bore,
And burst the boddice seams:

There, on the bosom as white as snow—
Daintily delicate, little and low,—
The blood-red crescent gleams!

'Yea, had I seen her,' the Wise One said,
'That day she crouched and covered her head
Beneath her mantle brown,
The innocent child had never been slain
To free yon fiend from the fatal chain
That drew her Hellwards down.

'Thoughtst thou to slip from the Devil's clutch,
Accursèd woman?—The laws for such,
Which Hell can ne'er unmake,
Give power to a draught of infant's blood—
When each new moon doth wake—
To shiver the spell of the signs that bud
Red as the incandescent flood
Of the ever-burning lake:
Though none can know what grief may grow
In other fashion of horrible woe,
For those who thus their fetters break.'

'Twas then there burst upon the ear,
Through the thick foliage far conveyed,

A mirthful joy-inspiring cheer,
That rippled like the waters clear
Of mountain torrents in the shade :

Methought that nature was released
From a terrific Demon's thrall.
Another cheer!—then signals ceased,
Forth from the thicket stepped a priest—
Our holy pastor, Padrê Paul.[30]

With many a smile and courteous bow
He waved his hat of margin wide,
Then wiped his ruddy, streaming brow,
And cast his cloak,—too heavy now,
Its woollen fabric purple-dyed.

'Well, well,' says he, 'what tasks require
Your Padrê in such haste to run?—
All smoking from my kitchen fire
A dish that hunger would inspire
In stomach of a saintly nun—
A dishful of the tenderest crows,
Stewed in a vinegar that knows
Its business! Scarce had I begun,

'When in comes Senhor Antony,
As frantic as a flustered quail;
"O Padrê! Padrê! haste," says he,
"Haste to the haunted Chestnut Tree!"
And then the fellow waxes pale,
And gasps as though his wind was spent:
So quick as weasel off I went,
Nor stopped to hear him tell the tale.

'Speak, sons!—unfold the honest truth.
Those knives at work again?—say true!
Well, well, one likes one's sport in youth.
—Saints! a dead woman?—Pshaw!—in sooth
There 's little here for me to do.'

He turned, and looked upon the corse
Reposing livid-lovely there;
And from it came a voiceless force
To strike a gazer with remorse
For evil thought of one so fair.

A while he mused in silentness,
Then from the Wise One answer sought—
Through what misfortune's direful stress,
Or stroke of vengeance pitiless,
The maiden to her doom was brought?

Not long ere to his pondering mind
The talė of mystery was told.
But what his thoughts we ne'er could find,
(To his own bosom all consigned,
A cave accustomed much to hold,)
Save this—That no one but a fool
Would trust a woman from that school
Replete with witchcrafts manifold,
Where Satan and his warlocks rule,—
Tarouca, in the mountains old.

'And now to business!' the Padrê cried:
'Carry the corpse to the bare hill-side,
And shovel it over with gravel stones;
The wild-cat and wolf at night will glide,
And swallow its flesh and crunch its bones.
Haste ye! haste ye!—then on, with a stride,
For work that is not meet for drones!

'Up with you, lads! we 'll away to the farm
And bury the infant, snug and warm,
Good ten foot deep in the clinging loam;
Thus keep ye yourselves and your flocks from harm,
When moonlight Vampires gibber and swarm,
When the accursêd Bruxas roam.[30]

'For lo! if the scent be once revealed
Of the corpse of an infant unaneled,
Unhallowed by Mass, and by priest unblest,—
The Bruxas come when the night prevails,
And they dig up the earth with their finger-nails
And drag the corpse from its place of rest.

'And ere they devour it, the hellish throng
Laughing and chuckling bear it along
Far to the heights of the desért hills;
Carry it off with a chant and a song,
Fouling the air with blightsome chills.
Then woe to the shepherd! and woe to the sheep
In the quiet fold on the mountain steep,
Lulled by the tinkle of pleasant rills,
Wrapt in the comfort of quiet sleep!
Over the shepherd they drag the dead
By the delicate cords of its twisted hair,
Over the sheep they trample and tread;
And wherever the corpse is lifted and led,
Death and destruction revel there,—
The poisonous corpse it murders and kills
With the tainted touch of its circling sweep

Faint were our hearts, our blood ran cold,
Fell Demons round us seemed to glide;

And some their beads of prayer o'ertold,
And some to Saints and Angels cried.
Straight the Chamorra's form we rolled
Within her mantle's sanguine fold,
And we left her on the bleak hill-side.
Then to the farm we swiftly hied,
And sank the infant in the mould.

'Here ends the tale I had to tell,'
The farmer said,—'the tale of blight.'
Thus had he kept his promise well,
And on his hearers laid a spell
To haunt them in the quiet night.

No words a while the silence broke;
Till, fain his mind to disenchant,
The English traveller lightly spoke,—
Said he, 'That maiden of the cloak
Was strange and fanciful, I grant,

'And certainly no simple dove:
But—in my native land at least—
Such symptoms are not thought to prove
A woman, beautiful as love,
To be a devil demi-beast!

'Now, Senhor, let me frankly own
That here I think your story fails—
'Tis really very far from shown
That the poor maiden, when o'erthrown
By those atrocious rusty nails,
Was not (good creature) there alone
To guard the babe from ills and ails.'

The farmer smiled,—then grave replies,
'The wolf stood manifest to view
Under the moonlight; in its eyes
I saw Joana's. All her lies
Could never make that fact untrue.

'Moreover, note the bludgeon-stroke
That struck the wolf so fair and flat,
And all its shoulder bruised and broke;
No gun-shot force the wound bespoke
That on Joana's shoulder sat,
Plain patterned by my sapling oak.
She never could account for that!'

The traveller answered,—'Such belief
The poet's fancy may employ;

But, in this universe of grief,
Our thought should never play the thief
And plunder us of hope and joy.

'Be these things verities indeed,—
Or be they such as men recite
Where old traditions live and breed
And mystery queens it in a creed,—
I dread not phantoms of the night;
Nor marvel much though bitter blight
'Gainst Earth's unsinning ones should speed;
Still shines the Everlasting Light,
And God the Inscrutable takes heed
To give to all things rightful meed—
Eternity sets all things right.'

THE MEDA MAIDEN.[31]

PART I.

THE MAIDEN.

WOODS among, when all was golden,
Autumnly and soft and olden,
In the pleasant Autumn time,—
Near the margin of a river,
Near the tawny ripplets' quiver,
Resting in her dreamy prime,

Sat a little Indian maiden,
Little rose-bud, sweetness laden,
Bright with dewy blooms of day;
Sat and sighed, and sadly pondered
O'er the hours so fast out-wandered,
Hours of childhood passed away;

Past and vanished like the breezes
Through a leafy wood—that seizes
  Hard their fleeting skirts, but holds
Nothing of them, saving greenness
From their softness, from their keenness
  Nought but deathly Autumn golds.

As she rested, vaguely musing,
In a childish dream confusing
  Thoughts of future, present, past;
Half her fancy backward turning,
Half outflown in anxious yearning
  Into realms of mystery cast;

As she sat in sunset splendour,
Near her sounded footsteps tender;
  Soon her kindly mother came,—
Came to her with fond caressing,
All her being breathing blessing,
  Breathing love's ethereal flame.

'Foolish child! I well might chide thee!'
Said the mother—'Wherefore hide thee
  Far from every anxious eye?
Nay, no answer!—such concealment
Makes to me a true revealment,
  Tells me that thine hour is nigh;

'Hour that bids thee—weary, fasting,
Earthly strength from off thee casting—
Pure to meet the Spirit hand;
Bids thee seek through hard probation
Power to help and heal thy nation,
Save thy home and native land.'

Counsels then she gave her daughter;
Secret lore she whispering taught her,
Well to note, as days went by,
Symbols shown on Nature's dial,
Warning signs to bide the trial,—
Winning live, or losing die.[33]

* * * *

Days went running, weeks went rolling,
Hungry frosts the earth controlling
Preyed on every pleasant thing;
Still the tender maiden rested,
Ne'er by mystic signs behested
Unto lonesome wandering.

* * * *

Woods among, when all was dreary,
Winterly, and whitely weary,
In the cruel Winter time,—
Where the snow lay smoothest, sleekest,
Where the wind was whistling bleakest,—
All her tresses flecked with rime,

Sat the little Indian maiden,
Soul and body overshaden,
 Wrapt in ghastly airs of gloom
Close and closer o'er her falling,—
Muffled voices round her calling,
 'Nerve thyself to meet thy doom.'

For the Undying Ones, preparing
Mortal frames for meetly bearing
 Sights and sounds of mystic day,
Move them first with dread o'erpowering,
Make them as the partridge cowering
 Shadowed by a bird of prey.

But, as sunshine enters, lighting
Darksome dells that fogs are blighting,
 Came the mother to her child ;
Led her back with soft compelling,
Till they neared the homely dwelling
 Whence she fled by fears beguiled.

'Neath the pine-trees old she stayed her ;
There a tiny lodge she made her,
 Bowered with branches closely pressed,
From the fragrant spruce-tree cloven,
Fixed and bound and interwoven,—
 Built her little one a nest.

'Here,' said she, 'my child, abide thou :
Here from every mortal hide thou :
  Earthly sustenance forego :
Hunger pangs, thou must endure them ;
Pains of thirst, thou must not cure them
  E'en by taste of purest snow.

'Guard thy soul from thoughts perplexing,
Fancies vagrant, terrors vexing,
  Wild impatience, chilling qualm ;
Souls perturbed by throng of notions
Loom too dense for heavenly motions—
  Heavenly Spirits move in calm.

'Now for two days' space I leave thee.
See! lest weary cares should grieve thee,
  Take that hatchet small of thine,
Fuel cut and store for burning ;
Rest thee then a while by turning
  Bass-wood bark to twisted twine.'

* * * * *

When the two days' space was ended
Through the woods the mother wended,—
  Found her blameless little one
Calmly working, still denying
Thirst's complaints and hunger's crying.
  Ah! she hoped her task was done!

Nay, 'twas yet the mere prolusion
Preluding a far conclusion—
Many a woeful chance between!
'To the child no hope is proffered,
Nought of sustenance is offered,
But, with sad and quiet mien,

Near herself the mother seats her,
Much commends her, much entreats her
All to suffer, all to prove.
'Once,' said she, 'my joys abounded;
Husband, daughters, sons, surrounded
Hearth and home with sheltering love.

'Gone, all gone, from earth departed,
Seized by Death the icy-hearted,
All save tender sisters three.
Cold our dwelling seems and dreary,
Maidens weak and mother weary—
Who shall care for them and me?

'Child! on thee I rest reliance:
Firm and faithful in compliance
Meet the peril, brave the strife.
Mark my words, and duteous hearken:
Fast thou still, thy features darken,
Bow before thy Lord of Life.[34]

'Fast thou truly; till with anguish
Heart grow cold and body languish;
  Thus that Lord shall see thy woe,
Look on thee with kind compassion,
Come to thee in mystic fashion,
  Secret marvels make thee know;

'Teaching thee in dream and vision
Purport of the high decision
  Spoke by him, that Spirit blest,
O'er thy Lord and all the master,—
What thy doom—to deep disaster,
  Or to joy's triumphal rest.'

* * * *

Counsel thus bestowed, the mother,
Tears of pity fain to smother,
  Rose and left her child alone;
But the maiden, strong of spirit,
Proved her title to inherit
  Blood of warriors stern as stone.[316]

Ne'er a sigh within her flutters,
Ne'er a murmuring word she utters,
  Silently she bears her pains,
Scorns the voice of hunger's raving,
Stills not thirst's more cruel craving,
  E'en from taste of snow refrains.

Patiently she plies her labours;
Viewless forms her only neighbours,
  Watching her with tireless eyes,
Prone to mark the least transgression,
Keen to hold her from possession
  Of the high prophetic prize.

Silent was the wood and wistful,
Strangled by the season tristful,
  Feebly longing, faintly fain,
Yearning for the Spring's arrival,
Reft of strength to make survival—
  Bound in Winter's rigid chain.

Hushed are all the forest voices,
Melody no more rejoices,
  Birds of music distant fled,—
Beauteous creatures still and sleeping,
Baneful creatures grimly creeping
  Like the phantoms of the dead.

Hushed the bittern's solemn booming,
Mounded snow his swamps entombing;
  Hushed the crane's discordant flute;
Hushed the night-jar's constant calling,
Rhythmic pulses rising, falling;
  All was desolate and mute.

Sight nor sound to scare the stillness,
Wake the woodland, cheer the chillness,
  Never on the senses broke;
Save the rare reverberation,
When with a crashing detonation
  Frost resistless ripped the oak.

* * * *

O'er the deserts unbefriended
Day his weary course had ended—
  Ended twice and sunk to night,—
Ere the maiden, sick and saddened,
By her mother's smile was gladdened,
  Strengthened by her looks of light.

But the mother, closely gazing,
Eyed her child, and fondly praising
  Blessed her for obedience true:
'Long,' she said, 'thou still must languish;
Ne'ertheless to ease thine anguish,
  See what now they bid me do!'

Straightway then she sets a tressel,
Kindles fire beneath a vessel,
  Melts the snow-flakes pure from soil;

Gives the child to drink,—but meagre
Is the draught, lest she, too eager
   Self to cheer, should lose her toil.

* * * *

Soon again the maid, deserted,
Patiently her powers exerted,
   Wood to sever, bark to cord:
Gracious Spirits round her wending
Saw her sorrows, and descending
   Strengthened her and brought reward;

Cleared her soul from earthly hazes,
Led her through celestial mazes,
   Ere the sixth day's night was old;
Showed her signs of wondrous glory,
Symbolised prophetic story,
   Words of mystic virtue told.

Now, the seventh day's sun appearing,
Whisper in the maiden's hearing
   Sounds that tell a joyous tale:
'Tis the mother, anxious speeding,
To her lonely child proceeding,
   Bearing food lest life should fail.

Ah! the body, long neglected,
Yields its right and lies dejected
 'Neath the soul's constraining power.
Soul, when stripped of earthly clothing,
Looks at earthly fare with loathing,
 Scorns what man and beast devour.

All the child's corporeal being,
Starved, had grown like soul in seeing,
 Hearing, power to taste and smell;
So sublimed and fine of essence
Scarce could she endure the presence
 Of her mother, loved so well.

* * * *

Homeward went the Indian woman:
Far from sights and voices human
 All alone the maid was left.
Then once more her axe she wielded;
Straight her faltering vigour yielded,
 Down she sank, of sense bereft.

Evening came: her sense recovered
Round her gracious Spirits hovered,
 Raised her soul and led it high,

Far above the earth's disorder,—
Led it upwards to the border
  Bounding heaven's transcendent sky.

Full with strength they likewise fraught her
When at morn her mother sought her,
  Coming in the early glow;
Nerved her to her want's relieving,
Sustenance for life receiving--
  Maize ensteeped in purest snow.

Gladly did the wistful mother
Watch the flame so nigh to smother—
  Life's fair flame—grow broad and bright.
'Child,' she said, 'thy Spirit-Master
Keeps thee safely from disaster,
  Leads thee to the mystic light.

'Say, my child, hath dream or vision
Taught thee true the dread decision
  Spoke by him, the Spirits' lord?
Nought concealing, tell me truly;
Thus my soul shall ponder duly,
  Weigh the Manito's award.'

Then the maiden—'Mother, hear me.
Evenings twain there wandered near me
  Spirits breathing airs that thrill;
And as darksome shades were falling
Softly came a sound of calling,
  Gentle as a distant rill.

'Mild was the voice as a rill that is running
Slow through the meadow-grass, stealthily shunning
Wafts of the wind that would ruffle its roaming,
Wilderness rocks that would fret it to foaming.
Musical, chill was the sound, as the breezes
Whirling the snow when it sparkles and freezes,
Dread in its gentleness, fateful and tender,
Moving in measures of rhythmical splendour.
" Come to me, maiden," the Spirit was crying,
" Thou in thy weakness so desolate lying;
Fainting and famishing, lonely and cheerless,
Come to me, child of the faithful and fearless!"

'I went to the voice: lo! a pathway was gleaming,
Like silver the track of its delicate beaming,
As cold as the northerly brightness that blazes
And fitfully dances in mystical mazes.
Far flashed the path, without winding or turning,
Straight to the stars in the firmament burning:

Upward and upward along it I glided,
Urged by the power that upheld me and guided.
Wan on my left a refulgence was lying,
Diffused by the sun in that hour of his dying;
Broad on my right broke a radiance incessant,
Cast by the moon from the crown of her crescent.
All-bright, where the rays were most widely expanding,
A woman majestic was movelessly standing.
Sacred she seemed as the Manito's daughter,
Round was her voice as the rolling of water,
Strong came her words, like the roar of a river:
"I am the Woman that liveth for Ever.[32a]
Thus am I named. With my name I endow thee;
Gifts for thy people, behold, I allow thee,—
Might o'er diseases, for quelling and curing—
Life to thee long among mortals enduring—
Life with the deathless in splendour eternal.
Go! thou art called to the glory supernal."

'Onward I went: then before me a being
Orb-like of body, most strange to the seeing,
Horns of the bison his forehead uprearing.
"Fear not," he said, as he viewed my appearing,
"List while I show thee the name I inherit—
'Tis Mônido-Wininees—Little Man-Spirit.[32b]

That is my life. In thy heart I enshrine it:
Boon for the first of thy sons I design it,
First of the sons that as mother shall love thee.
Onwards! proceed to the regions above thee!"

'—Upward and upward—till, far in the heaven,
There oped a wide door in the firmament riven.[32c]
Thence came a voice, and I stopped, and I listened.
Near to my path stood a Spirit that glistened!
O'er his broad breast was a vestment befleckered,
Azurely tinted, and silverly chequered.
Round his fair head was a halo of splendour
Darting bright glory-beams ruddy and slender.
"Look at me, child," said the Spirit immortal;
"I am the veil of the firmament's portal.[32d]
Fear not, O maiden, but rest thee and hearken.
Labours and sorrows thy daylight shall darken;
Ne'er shall they quell thee, nor sorely dismay thee:
Lo, in the strength of my life I array thee."

'Suddenly, spear-points around me were shining;
They clung to my body like serpents' entwining,
Painlessly pressed me, then earthwards descended;
Oft they returned ere the trial was ended.

"Wait thou a while," said the Spirit, "I mete thee
Trial more mighty to arm and complete thee."
Then came a storm of keen arrow-heads, clinking
Hard on my bosom, and wounding and sinking;
Painlessly piercing me, swiftly withdrawing,
They melted and vanished like icicles thawing.
"Lo!" said the Spirit, "the work is completed:
Fulness of days as thy portion is meted.
Gaze through yon rift in the firmament broken:
Further advance not—thy limit is spoken.
Take thou my name, in thy heart I enfold it;
Thine to bestow, or for ever to hold it.
Child, it is time unto Earth to repair thee:
Yonder is he that is waiting to bear thee."

'Then at my side moved a marvellous creature,
Snake-like of body and wolf-like of feature.
"Fear thou not, child," said the Spirit of splendour,
"Fear not to fly with the Comet's attender."
Straight on the back of the serpent reclining,
Swiftly it bore me as light in its shining,
Meteor-like flashing and rushing and gleaming,
All my long locks like a thunder-cloud streaming.
Swift as the lightning it earthwards descended:
Alone was I left:—and my vision was ended.

'Thus the first night—thus the second.
Forth I wandered, heavenward beckoned,
Saw the Woman stand on high,
Saw the Man with horns of bison,
Saw beside the heaven's horizon
Him that rules the bright blue sky.

'Selfsame words again were spoken,
Same were trial, sign, and token,
Gracious gift and glorious meed,—
Names of might and mystery granted,
Endless life within me planted;—
Same the wondrous serpent-steed.

'Voices hushed and sights departed,
Lone I lay, and weary-hearted
Watched the moon her course complete.
Lo! I saw a meteor falling,
Dark and round; which, strangely crawling
Poised on human hands and feet,

'Left the place whereon it lighted,
Sought me (marv'lling, ne'er affrighted),
Shrieked, more shrill than whistling blast,
"Child! I give thee gifts prophetic,
Power to seize with might magnetic
Mysteries present, future, past."

'Then it rose, with sudden springing,
Birdlike wings asunder flinging,
High above its head upreared—
Ruddy head of bird that rattles
Hard on hollow oaks, and prattles,
Shrieks with laughter wild and weird.'[32e]

Thus the maiden told her story.
Said the mother—'Stars of glory
Far up yonder gleam and glow:
Not more fair those lights above thee
Shine, than lights which those who love thee
Bring to deck thee here below.

'Three days wait, my child, remaining
Lonely here, from food refraining.
So the Spirits shall record
Perfect all thy work and finished.
Ne'er undone to be, nor minished,
Work's desert or work's reward.'

Firm and true, the faithful maiden,
Burden-bearer largely laden,
Sought not from her fate to roam.
Three days pass, then swift returning
Comes the mother, weeping, yearning,
Brings her loved one joyous home.

Drums were beaten, songs resounded,
Warriors feasted, mirth abounded;
  Priests unto the maid drew near,
Called her to the Jeesukâwin,
Called her to the high Medâwin,
  Hailed her prophetess and seer.[35]

* * * *

Thrice had Winter deathward wandered,
Summers four their wealth had squandered,
  Dwined and shivered, fainted, died;
Lo, once more renewed to vigour,
Winter ramps with ruthless rigour,
  Quelling joys at every stride.

Near the Wisacoda River—
True and loyal tribute-giver
  To the glorious western sea,
Gitchi-gumee, Lake Superior,
King of kingly lords inferior,
  Vast in aqueous sovereignty,

Where the Wisacoda slumbered,
Frost-benumbed and ice-encumbered,
  Deep within the forest's space,
Screened by many a pine-tree steeple,—
Dwelt the Meda-maiden's people,
  Dwelt the proud Ojibway race.[36]

Ah! what grief a nation crushes
O'er whose being Famine rushes,
  Fells his victim, holds him tight;
Babes and mothers weeping, wailing,
Old men dying, young men failing,
  Hope's last sunshine turned to night.

Groaning thus in grim starvation
Bides the proud Ojibway nation:
  Tireless hunters toil in vain,
Fruitlessly their quest they vary,
Search the woodland, search the prairie,
  Search the lifeless wood and plain.

'Twas the hour when day was dying,
Silent in her home was lying,
  Musing still, the Meda-maid;
Slowly then the doorway curtain
Opened, and the light uncertain
  Showed a form in robes arrayed.

Chieftain he, in power excelling:
To the gentle maiden's dwelling
  Came he, seeking aid most high;
Urged the mother, much besought her,
Firm of heart to warn her daughter
  Help to summon from the sky.

* * * *

Lo, 'tis noontide: Spirit-meted,
See the temple stands completed,
  Prophet's-lodge, of fabric strong,—
Ten tall posts of diverse timber,
Circled close with moose-skin limber,
  Tightly tied with many a thong.[37]

All is finished. Firm and steady,
See, the sacred lodge is ready,
  Dight for guests that soon will come:
See, the maiden enters—closes
Fast the door—then low reposes,
  Crouches, chants, and beats her drum:

Calling with the sound persistent
Spirits near and Spirits distant
  Pledged to come at her behest:
Calling the Eternal Woman;
Calling Him of aspect human
  With the hornêd bison crest;

Calling to the earthlier essence,
Forest bird in form and presence
  Or as meteor rolling round;
Calling measuredly and lowly,
Drumming solemnly and slowly,
  Prostrate on the quiet ground.[38]

Solemnly she chants and slowly
Meda music high and holy,
Drear as voice of desert airs;
Wild she screams the chorus olden,
Wolfish wailing long upholden,
Moaning of the mountain bears.

'At the place of light,
At the end of the sky,
I (the Great Spirit)
Come and hang
Bright sign,
A! a! a!—Ha!—aha!

'At the sound of my voice
(My prophet-voice)
I shake my lodge
(By hands unseen),
My sacred lodge.
A! a! a!—Ha!—aha!

'Haih! the weird white bird!
He flies round clouds and skies—
He sees (unspeakable sight!)
Around the clouds and skies—
By his clear eyes I see—I see—I know!
A! a! a!—Ha! aha!'[39]

Suddenly, with sounds of rushing
Surged a tide of influence, flushing
O'er the lodge, which heaved and swayed
Through the magic all-controlling:
Then the Spirit round and rolling
Moved before the Meda-maid.

Silent lay the maiden, ending
Beat of prophet-drum, attending
  Question urged by priest and chief.
And they said—'With much beseeching,
Famine-struck, we sue for teaching
  Where to find our want's relief.'

'Ha, ha, ha! ye nation blinded,'
Shrieked the Spirit, mirthful-minded,
  'Eyes so bad are much to blame!
Where the sunny flood is flowing,
O'er the western prairie glowing,
  Stronger eyes would mark their game.'

* * * *

Ere the morning moved in glory
Through the forest high and hoary,
  Forth the ardent hunters sped:
Westward, westward, still they wended;
Joyously their task was ended
  Ere the evening light was fled.

Lordly moose were slain, and carried
O'er the snow to those that tarried
  Halting on their hunters' track;
Sighted on the far horizon,
Moved a mighty band of bison,
  Surged a bellowing sea of black.

Farewell famine! farewell sorrow!
Food to-day and feast to-morrow!
  Withered life has waxen green.
Mothers weep away their sadness,
Children leap and laugh with gladness,
  Ancient warriors smile serene.

Hearts beat gaily, mirth abounded,
Songs re-echoed, drums resounded:
  To the Meda-maid drew nigh
Priestly chiefs, and made oration,
Hailed her hope of all the nation,
  Hailed her prophetess most high.

PART II.

THE WIFE.

TWELVEMONTHS four with fortunes laden
Looked upon the Meda-maiden,
Wandered out their days, and died.
Now the virgin sweet and slender
Yields to music soft and tender,
Wooed to be a warrior's bride—

Strong-Sky,[32]—bold of heart and bearing,
Hunter skilful, swift, and daring.
Loving lived they summers three;
Blissful time beyond all telling,
Peace and plenty cheered her dwelling,
Children danced upon her knee.

Ah! when Fortune smiles the fairest
Oft she strips a bosom barest,
Meet for thrusts that none can brave;
Poison-darts that cut most keenly
'Light on those that live serenely,
Heedless of the gaping grave:

Thus the maiden—now the *woman*,—
Human aid nor superhuman
Saves her from the fated blow.
'Twas the time when trees were budding,
Snow departing, rivers flooding,—
Then befell her weary woe.

Far from wonted wood and prairie,
Nigh the village of St. Mary
Where the huckstering white men stayed,
Strong-Sky set his habitation,
Scarce a bowshot from the station
Rich in goods for truck and trade.

Day by day, with packs of peltry
Goes he to the storehouse sweltry,
Fain to barter fur-goods fair—
Mellow marten, mink, and beaver,
Wolverine and wolf the reaver,
Fox and fisher, lynx and bear.

There he waits in calm endurance,
All the traders' trained assurance
Weak to bend his patient will,
Juggling him with artful measures,
Tempting him with tawdry treasures,—
Firm of purpose rests he still.

Vain an Indian trader's trouble
Proff'ring with deception double
  Guileful goods and measures spare;
Wiser, with deception single,
Godliness and gain to mingle—
  Guileful goods but measures fair.

Wiser, till the fiery liquor
Cause the light of sense to flicker
  In the wary wild-man's brain;
Then, bereft of will and reason,
Helpless lies he for a season,
  Gluts the trader full with gain.

Gaultier now—a trader's brother,
Half-breed, of Ojibway mother,
  Fraught with twofold types of wrong
(Vice of Frenchman, vice of savage),
Apt for murder, theft, and ravage,
  Foul and fickle, false of tongue,—

Gaultier, skilled in sly evasions,
Works on Strong-Sky with persuasions,
  Begs a visit to his tent,
Where at night a jovial party,
Boon companions blithe and hearty,
  Meet for friendly merriment.

'Go not,' said his wife, 'I pray thee,
Gaultier flatters to betray thee.'
Haughty souls are hard to melt,
Forth he fared, her counsel scorning.
Then the Seeress wafts of warning
Deep within her spirit felt.

Mystic beings round her fluttered,
Mystic voices mournful muttered,
'Follow, follow on his track!
Fast the fateful hours are flying,
Hasten, hasten,—weeping, sighing,
Woo thy heedless husband back.'

Swift she followed, and besought him.
More to rage than ruth she wrought him,
Ruin bent: she sued in vain.
Strong-Sky on his way proceeded,
Heavenly warnings all unheeded:
Homeward then she turned again.

Men too vagrant oft make merry,
Leaving wives at home to bury
Perished joy 'mid silence drear:
Hours the Meda-woman waited,
Midnight came, yet ne'er abated
Cruel stress of deadly fear.

Then a while her anguish ended.
Worn and weary she had tended
  Motherly her ailing child;
Sleep unsought her body captured,
Stole away her soul,—enraptured,
  Far from earthly scenes beguiled.

Rude and rueful is her waking!
Breathless comes a maiden, shaking
  Her who slumbers calm at home.
'Haste!' the maiden's voice is calling,
'Haste to Gaultier's, ere their brawling
  Turn to mischief. Come, oh come!'

Up the dreary, flooded river,—
Like to birds whose pinions quiver
  Swift through shades of darkness sent,
Knowing neither pause nor error,—
Fleet they onward in their terror
  Till they reach the Half-breed's tent.

Still—all still!—as when the thunder
Rests, ere, rending skies asunder,
  Lightning leaps with lurid light—
All was silent, sad, and lonely,
Nought within the tent, save only
  Leaden-weighted glooms of night.

Fain the Meda-wife would quicken
Fire from trampled embers, stricken
Deep into the oozy clay:
Hopeless—though she toil for ever.
Forth, once more, along the river
Mournfully she made her way.

Clouds departing, light grows clearer;
On the ground she sees anear her
Tiny gleams as if from glass;
Then the moonlight, faintly shimmering,
'Neath the speck of radiance glimmering
Showed a black and quiet mass.

Strong-Sky?—yea: she knew the shining
Trinket that he wore. Reclining
Sidelong laid he seemed to sleep.
Tow'rds the slumberous figure bending
Stooped his weary wife, intending
Vigil o'er his rest to keep.

Suddenly, her footstep slipping
Through the herbage dank and dripping,
Prone upon her knees she fell.
What is this!—her hands are bloody.
Ah! the tokens rankly ruddy
Told the dreadful tale too well.

There, beneath the moonlight hoary,
Strong-Sky rested, stark and gory,
  Hewed with hatchet, hacked with knife.
With her loving hand the woman
Stroked his face, the chill inhuman
  Froze away all hopes of life.

Will she faint? or frenzied flying
Leave the loathly body lying,
  Food for wolf that wandering preys?
Firm of heart when fate is sorest
Bide the children of the forest,—
  Tearless by the corpse she stays.

'Neath the night-cloud's cheerless awning
Bides she, till the wings of dawning
  Flap the sky with gusty chill;
Bides she, till the orb of splendour
Comes with comfort warm and tender,
  While the birds in chorus trill:

Bides and bides in sad quiescence;
Scarce aware of mortal presence
  E'en when many round her wait—
Hardy soldiers, rough and ready,
Stern officials, staid and steady,
  Summoned from the Fort—too late.

Hours too late—the evil doers,
Jesting at their slow pursuers,
  Far from vengeful law had fled.
Scanty grudge the white men cherished,
'Twas an Indian that had perished:
  So, to rid them of the dead,

Strong-Sky's corpse they raised, and carried
To the Indian folk that tarried
  Nigh the Fort's stockaded wall;
These among their graves ancestral
Laid him, 'neath the flowers campestral,
  Where the roaring waters fall.

But the Seeress, sorrow-stricken,
Filled with terrors vague, that sicken
  Firmest souls by anguish rent,
Took her infants twain, and speeded,
All unheeding and unheeded,
  To a lonely forest-tent

Where her mother old was staying.
News of ill makes no delaying:
  Faster than the Seeress fled
Winged its way the tale of slaughter;
Mournful mother, mournful daughter,
  Met with moanings o'er the dead.

Soon her ancient blood heroic,
Boon from many a forest stoic—
Blood of Waubojeeg the sire,[316]
Waubojeeg the great in story—
Woke the Seeress with its glory,
Warmed her icy veins with fire.

High her dròoping head she lifted,
Wiped away the tears that drifted
Down her chill and haggard cheeks,
Quelled the sobs she scarce could smother:
Then, for solace to her mother,
Thus with patient voice she speaks:—

'Mourn not that which hath betided,
By the All-ruling Spirit guided
Moves the good or moves the ill:
Joyful in the love remaining,
O'er the lost no more complaining,
Humbly let us wait his will.'

Said the careworn mother, weeping,
'Soon *my* sorrow would be sleeping—
But for thee, my child, I moan.
Sad those days when I—forsaken,
All my help and comfort taken,
Husbandless and poor and lone—

('Lone—though, 'neath my tent-skins lying,
Infants for their food were crying)—
Lonely toiled, with none to aid!
Soon, my earthly ways outwended,
Death will take me: then unfriended
Thou shalt labour, faint, and fade.'

But the Seeress answered, 'Near me
Spirits wait to help and cheer me.
Though I walk in weary ways—
Sorrows many, pleasures scanted—
Yet the All-ruling Lord hath granted
Long continuance of my days.

'Fear not, hope not, all is ordered;
Fenced my lodge of life, and bordered
Surely by the streams of fate.
Lo, my mystic eyes, unshrouded,
Clear have looked on lands unclouded,
Never more can Earth seem great.'

Long conversing each with other
Sat the daughter and the mother.
When the hours of night were o'er
Far they fared, and made their dwelling
Where the watery waste was swelling
Wide on Gitchi-gumee's shore.

* * * *

Three years dwelt the Seeress single,
Ere by warrior wooed to mingle
Fates with him as duteous bride—
Fair-Cloud[32g] he by name. She bore him
Daughters two. Then coldly o'er him
Breathed grim Pauguk,[32h] and he died.

Far were they from friends abiding,
Leagues of wilderness dividing
Widowed wife and orphan band,
Lonely left, from all their nation—
Camped in Winter habitation
Nigh the frozen river's strand.

Yielded then the Seeress, weakly,
To the blast that blew so bleakly,
Withering wan her spirit's bloom?
Lay she frantic and despairing,
Bosom beating, tresses tearing,
Crushed beneath that heavy doom?

Nay: such ecstasies of grieving,
Potent for a soul's relieving
Restfully in quiet placed,
Serve not well in times more urgent,
Serve not well for those emergent
Starving from a desert waste.

Stern came grief; she sternly met it;
Silent raised the corpse, and set it
  Firmly on its coffin low—
Hearse and bier—a hand-sled tender,
Lath of fir-wood slim and slender,
  Meet for gliding o'er the snow.

Over all with spirit heedful
Store she lays of things most needful,
  Food, and robe for nightly bed;
On her back the babes she places,
Sets their brethren to the traces,
  With them drags the weighty sled.

'Mong the wintry forest shadows,
Through the lonely beaver-meadows,
  Music'd by the Wood-wolf's howl;
O'er the prairie white and speckless,
Where against the azure fleckless
  Statued stands the Snowy Owl;[32i]

Steadfast went they, onward keeping,
Children working, babies sleeping,
  Mother toiling wan as death;
Daily when the sun was glowing,
Nightly when the moon was throwing
  Chillness on the icy path,

Onward, onward, still they wended;
Heavenly powers their steps attended,
  Sheltering wings around them cast,
Nerved their bodies to endurance,
Filled their hearts with firm assurance,
  Led them to their home at last.

Thus a woman's faithful spirit
Caused dead Fair-Cloud to inherit
  Best of goods that corpse may crave:
Funeral trophies, rites and honours,
Tributes paid by liberal donors,
  Rest in the ancestral grave.[32j]

* * * *

Years rolled on; and ever flowing
Waxed the sea of sorrow, throwing
  Waves that chill the fervent blood
O'er the fated woman's being—
Peace departing, pleasure fleeing,
  Banished by the bitter flood.

Death comes nigh, and slowly slaying,
Strikes her first-born son, delaying
  Deep to drive the cruel dart;
Day by day she sees him languish,
Day by day a mother's anguish
  Rends her fond and faithful heart.

Lo, one eve, his pains beguiling,
Slumber came. He wakened smiling,
  Glory glinting from his eyes.
Then the mother's soul unfailing
Knew his spirit had been sailing
  Far beyond the earthly skies.

'Oh, my son,' she said, 'what glory
Lingers here? Thy vision's story
  Canst thou, wilt thou, dare to speak?'
'Mother,' said the young man, 'truly
Small my hope to answer duly
  What thou askest—words are weak.

'Through a storm-cloud dark and dreary
Passed I to the great blue prairie
  O'er whose face the stars are spread;
Far away there rolled a water
Black of hue, methought a daughter
  Born from fountains of the dead.

'Fast I flitted o'er that river—
Stream of smoothness—ripple, quiver,
  Ne'er its turbid current broke:
Through a forest next I wended,
Wild-wood greenly twined and blended,
  Pine and poplar, fir and oak.

'Broad beneath me then a valley:
There in many a blooming alley,
 There by many a lovely brook,
Moved the deer and stately bison,
Swans and beauteous birds that dizen
 All on which the eye can look.

'Near me, in a balsam thicket,
Stood a hut with wall and wicket:
 Forth there comes an agêd sire;
White his locks, across his shoulder
Hangs a robe of skins, no colder
 Gleam his eyes than flame of fire.

'Leaning on a staff he waited.
Scarce had I—mine awe abated—
 Mastered words my tale to tell,
Ere his voice came low and thrilling;
"Nay," said he, "a welcome willing
 Take from one who loves thee well.

'"Rest a while, for strength's sustaining,
Long the journey yet remaining."
 Gladly to his hut I went.
Rested, by the door he guides me,
Through the wood-wall that divides me
 Straitly from the vale's descent.

'Down the rocky steep I wended,
Following on a track that trended
  Crosswise o'er the valley green,
Down the brooks that thread the bowers,
Past the beauteous birds and flowers,
  Past the creatures mild of mien.

'There a power mysterious speeds me;
Rock nor forest-tree impedes me,
  Clearly through them glides my soul,
Earthly substance left behind me,
Safe with him who thus consigned me
  Body-free to seek my goal.

'Lo, at length a lake unbounded;
Lo, a lovely land surrounded
  All ways by its crystal tide;
Near me, moored on shores of brightness
Rests a fair canoe, whose whiteness
  Gleams upon the waters wide—

'Wondrous craft, of marble seeming,
Marble paddles in it gleaming
  Deftly fashioned for the hand:
In I stepped, and swiftly flying
O'er the waters limpid lying,
  Sought to gain the island's strand.

'Ere the midway flood I breasted,
Rushed great billows foamy-crested
  Fiercely tow'rds my fair canoe;
Swelled and surged the lofty billows,
Round as prairie-groves of willows
  Reared against the cloudless blue.

'Swelling, surging, heaving, dashing,
Hurling breakers broadly flashing,
  Burst the waves in blinding spray;
Foaming whirlpools, reckless wreathing
Garlands wrought from milky seething,
  Swirled around my witless way.

'Ne'ertheless, through drift and drearness
Yet the water holds its clearness:
  Down, far down, in purple deeps,
Gray on sand-beds dimly golden
Glimmered corpses new and olden,
  Skeletons in heaps on heaps.

'All the while anear me glided
Bright canoe-craft marble-sided,.
  Man or woman each one bore;
Over them the waters surging
One by one in ruin merging,
  Down they sank, and rose no more.

'Scatheless some were fleetly flitting
Through the breakers, in them sitting
  Children fair and sweet to see;
Ne'er a bark with man or woman
'Scaped the water's wrath inhuman,
  'Scaped the vengeful glassy sea.

'Then I cried, "The waters crave me,
Vengeance threatens; who shall save me?
  How shall I these waves endure!"
Loud a lordly voice came, calling—
"Heed not foul things ruined falling:
  True art thou, and brave, and pure."

'Straightway all my fears are banished,
Harmlessly the billows vanished
  Ere they touched my bright canoe,
Breaking like the rainbowed bubble:
Safe beyond the tempest's trouble
  O'er the waters wide I flew.

'Fast as flies the war-bird's fleetness
Wend I to the isle of sweetness,
  Land upon its lovely shore;
Balmy breezes warm and tender
Breathe upon my soul, and render
  Force of life in endless store.

'Forest creatures fair and loving
Deck the lilied prairies, moving
Softly through the gentle flowers,
Cold and hunger all unknowing,
Pain and fear no shadow throwing
Sadly on their sunlit hours.

'Then, methought, "This isle of sweetness
For my soul hath wondrous meetness,
Here for ever let me dwell.
Far from pain and toil and sorrow,
Glad to-day and glad to-morrow,--
Yea, this island suits me well."

'Calmly came an influence, stealing
Through my spirit, clear revealing
One who stands in glory dread;
Mild of aspect, grave and tender,
Bright his body gleams with splendour,
Golden thorns are round his head.

'On mine eyes his eyes are gazing,
Every sense in marvel mazing;
Neither can I speak nor move;
But the glory of his glances
Lovingly my being trances,
All my heart is steeped in love.

'Ne'er a word his lips are speaking;
Spirit unto spirit seeking,
  Mine he seeks with his to fill;
Found, he thrills me through with yearning,
Then into himself returning
  Leaves me conscious of his will.

'Thus his spirit spake: "I tell thee
None shall harm thee, nought shall quell thee,
  Blended with the Lord of Life.
Trust not powers of earthly being,
Spirits earth-bound, dark of seeing,
  Weak to shield thy soul in strife.

'"Forth unto thy mother speed thee;
Speak my words, her soul shall heed thee,
  Messenger of peace and truth.
Surely will I seek and find her,
Surely will I take and bind her
  Close with cords of love and ruth."

'Then that Blest One (thus methought me)
Bade me kneel, and spirits brought me
  Robe as pure as mountain snows.
This the lordly Master places
Over me, it all embraces,
  Over all my being flows.

'"Mine thou art" (methought he spake it),
"Robed thou art, for symbol take it
Mine thou art to hold for aye."
Mist-clouds then my soul pervaded,
Brightness vanished, sweetness faded;
Cold I woke to earthly day.'

* * * *

Ere that night its hours had numbered
Wakelessly the young man slumbered,
Hushed by him of icy hand:
Body, earth with earth, abided;
Soul and spirit, angel-guided,
Hasted to the Happy Land.[32k]

Part III.

THE CHRISTIAN.

Dreary is the purple heaven,
Dark when o'er its moon is driven
  Solemn clouds that quell the light;
Dreary was the Meda's dwelling,
Dark with clouds beyond dispelling,
  Reft of him that made it bright.

Glorious are the worlds of pleasure
Garnered in that priceless treasure—
  Gold of gold—a lovely son:
Ghastly are the worlds of sorrow
Garnered in the mother's morrow •
  When his earthly day is done.

Now the Meda's pride will languish,
Softened in the seas of anguish;
  More of woe she scarce can need.
Ne'ertheless, with sad renewal
Yet must come the tear bedewal,
  Deadlier yet her heart must bleed.

Soon, ah! soon, the hapless mother
Yields unto the grave another
  Well-belov'd—a daughter young.
Now indeed is time revealing
Marvels hid by mystic sealing,
  Secrets told in mystic tongue.

Now her memory wakes, recalling
Darts and arrows round her falling,
  Wounding sore in wondrous ways;
Seen and felt in childhood's vision,
Sequel to the high decision
  Dowering her with length of days;

Now indeed, with spirit broken,
Marketh she in this a token
  Figured in the sacred sky,
Sign of pangs to grieve her hoarded—
Crucial meed to souls awarded
  Held by Heaven in favour high.

Dazed and crushed, perception clouded,
All her light in darkness shrouded,
  Weary seemed unearthly lore;
Deep within her welled a yearning—
Oh! for pathway for returning
  Back to commonness once more!

Strong within her memory working,
Clear among the fancies lurking
Dimly scattered one by one,
Comes the thought of Him of glory,
Robe-bestower in the story
Visioned to her dying son.

Truly for her wounded spirit
Much that memory held of merit,
Strangely full with comfort fraught:
Yet of Him with brows enfolden
Fair with thorny garlands golden,
Save in picture knew she nought.

Oft o'er seas of dire distresses
Shines a sudden gleam, that blesses
Soothingly as angel's song;
E'en as if by fateful tractions
Evils drew their counteractions
Strongly as themselves were strong.

Thus the Meda's drearest trouble
Issues soon in comfort double,
Joy o'er past and future laid;
Comfort brought by one who carried
Gospel grace to those that tarried
Darkly in the heathen shade;

Brought by one of Indian nation,
Bearing news of Christ's salvation—
  Strong to scatter Satan's mist:
Grand Ojibway name forsaken,[32]
Homely name the man had taken,
  "Sunday, the Evangelist."

'Ho!' he cries, 'ye weak and weary,
Sorry-hearted, sick and dreary,
  Come to Christ and find your rest;
Come for raiment brightly shining,
Cast away the robes of pining,
  Cast the trouble from your breast.

'Trust no more in ghostly creatures—
Evil things of bestial features,
  Creeping things of sin and shame:
Totems, scrolls of conjuration,
Rattles, drums of invocation,
  Hurl them into flood and flame.

'Come to Christ, the high and holy,
Come to Christ, the meek and lowly,
  Lord of lords and Light of light:
Though your souls be grimed and gory,
Yield them to the Lord of glory,
  He shall make them pure and white.

'See yon azure vast and spacious!
Lo, that Lord, the good, the gracious,
  Dwelling far above yon sky,
Left His home in lands unclouded,
Came in humble form enshrouded,
  Came to earth to grieve and die.

'Fear not! fear not! bring your sorrow;
Wait not for the weak to-morrow,
  Death companions fear and doubt.
Come to Christ with strong beseeching,
Come for comfort, come for teaching;
  None that cometh casts He out.'

Thus the preacher spake, and truly
Hearkened one who heard him duly;
  All her soul was open thrown;
Softened by the streams of grieving
Tender was it for receiving
  Sacred seed so meetly sown.

How she prays, all else neglected,
Craves to know her soul elected,
  Safe with Christ in heavenly love!
How in lonely supplication
Cries she for a revelation
  Visioned from the Lord above!

Ne'er a dream nor vision taught her:
Needed not—God's Spirit sought her,
  Bathed her heart with balm of peace,
Soothed away her anxious yearning;
Lovely lights within her burning
  Darksome terrors fade and cease.

Ah! in vain shall souls benighted,
Lapt in earth, benumbed and blighted,
  Arbitrate on heavenly grace:
While they talk of times and seasons,
Primly prate of rules and reasons,
  Keep religion in its place,—

Forth the Spirit flows, and flushes
Deeply o'er a soul, and hushes—
  Whelmed beneath the sacred flood—
All the clang of reason's raving,
All the sigh of fleshly craving
  Murmuring treason in the blood.

Then the soul, in waiting wonder,
Thinks to hear Jehovah's thunder:
  Lo, it hears a still, small voice,
Softly through its silence ringing,
Sweetly solemn, singing, singing,
  'Love, and worship, and rejoice.'

So the Seeress, new-created,
Pagan pride for ever bated,
  Greets the incoming Spirit's power;
Yields herself with meek surrender,
Garners up the influence tender,
  Grows in glory hour by hour.

Soon before the congregation
Makes she Christian attestation,
  Sealed by water's witnessing:
Ne'er the Evangelist refuses
Hallowed rites to one that chooses
  Christ for Saviour, Priest, and King.

Heaven within her heart enshrining
Welcomes she the waters, signing
  Advent of the Sacred Flame:
Passes then her olden title—
Change to mate with change more vital—
  Katharine now becomes her name.

Gone is all her heathen glory;
Gone the grace of forests hoary,
  Gone the sweetness of the flower,
Gone the mystic Meda splendour,
Gone the radiance wildly tender
  Gleaming in her eyes of power.

Changed, all changed. Her movement stately
Falters now, she moves sedately,
  Meekly musing as she goes;
All her spirit's novel beauty,
Cramped in iron bonds of duty,
  Outwardly no token shows.

Gone is all her brave apparel,
Bright with beads that seemed to carol
  Choruses of Nature's song:
Gone the garb of rare devices,
Snowy-white, with paradises
  Blooming quaintly all along.[32m]

Sober now her dress and gown-like,
Dull, and dim, and dark, and town-like.
  —O ye Christian people wise!
Comes your creed from darksome regions
Fraught with sad, despairing legions?
  Comes it not from heavenly skies?

Wherefore should your joyful tidings
Bring the outward signs of chidings
  Grievously by sinners borne?
Know ye not that Christ is risen,
Wherefore haunt ye then the prison
  Reft by Him in glorious scorn?

All things beauteous, all things winning,
All that shames the shade of sinning,
  Take them as the Christian's own;
Hues of early Eden bowers,
Hues of forests, fields, and flowers,
  Take them as the Lord's alone.

Work not with the huckstering spirits,
Foes to all that man inherits
  Holiest from the primal scheme,—
Felling forests, sullying rivers,
Fouling every breeze that quivers,
  (Dragon-like) with fetid steam.

Curses on the gropers greedy,
Spoilers of the poor and needy!—
  Poor and needy? Yea, MANKIND:
Needy for the want of sweetness,
Needy for the want of meetness,
  Plundered by these locusts blind.

O ye Christian folk, be wary,
Tender-souled, discreetly chary,
  When with heathen folk ye deal;
Heed not infant superstitions,
Stickle not at babe traditions,—
  Break not wood-flies on the wheel.

Leave the lesser weeds agrowing,
Sweet perchance though strangely blowing,
  Sure your garden wants not space!
Many a weed by care in tending
Blooms to beauty in the ending;
  Spare small faults to save great grace.

—Nay, too fast my pen is speeding
Truth cries out, 'A spell of weeding
  Lacks that flowery page—go to!
Fantasies, imaginations,
Tangled up with plain narrations,
  Turn to falsehood half the true.'

Humbly then I make confession,
Own my warrantless digression
  Wandering forth beyond the pale
Builded by my grave narrator,
Honest-minded, no creator
  Fashioning a specious tale.[31a]

Nought he notes the Meda's bearing,
Nothing tells of garment-wearing,
  Little save of change of name:
Ne'ertheless (too well I know it,
Thousand thousand stories show it,
  Thousand travellers speak the same),

Well 'tis known that priests and preachers,
Zealous-minded Christian teachers
Hard with Heathendom at strife,
Oft, in guise of sacred duty,
Murder mirthfulness and beauty,
Slay the gracefulness of life.

Thus, with candour undiminished,
Reckon I of him that finished
What good "Sunday" had begun ;[32n]
Find that much his words betoken
Bands of stately custom broken,
Bands of vulgar custom spun :

Many a phrase of trivial figure
Volumes into books of vigour,
Viewed by one that closely heeds.
—Pass we now to matters certain,
Hidden 'neath no veiling curtain,
Published of the Meda's deeds.

This we learn : she straight dismisses,
Relegates to hell's abysses,
All the Spirits of the shade ;
All the wondrous, weirdly beings
Oft revealed in mystic seeings,
Ever nigh to cheer and aid.

Straight she brings the records painted[40]—
Honoured once, but now attainted—
  Bright with figures painted clear,
Hieroglyphs of hidden learning
Known to none but souls discerning,
  Sacred knowledge of the seer;

. .

Shows the symbols of Medâwin,
Shows the signs of Jeesukâwin,[35]
  Tells a white man all the tale;
Sings the songs of might magnetic,
Seekers of the sight prophetic,
  Songs to sing behind the vail.[39]

Christian candour much applauded,
Christian conduct much belauded,—
  So her grave historian saith:[31a]
Thus she shines as saint converted,
Direful practices deserted,
  League dissolved with Hell and Death.

.

Be it so,—yet well consider,
Ye who fain had joined to bid her
  Ban each kindly spirit-friend;
Pause, and ponder well this question,
Wholesome for the soul's digestion:—
  Where doth God's dominion end?

Rules He hell, and earth, and heaven?
Or hath sway supreme been riven,
  Somewhere, from His hands divine?
Nay: no thought of swiftest pinion
Wends to empire whose dominion
  God hath chosen to resign.

Mark ye, therefore!—men, or angels;
Christians fair in bright evangels;
  Heathens dark in ghostly dearth;
Grewsome fiends abhorred by mortals;
Dubious dwellers 'twixt the portals
  Closing heaven and closing earth;—

All as God's own creatures greeting,
Equal rule to all outmeeting,
  Thus we judge the eternal brood:
That which doeth ill is evil,
Be it angel, man, or devil;
  That which doeth good is good.

Mark you then the woodland haunters,—
You, O man whose spirit saunters
  Dozing on the beaten track;
Ponder well their interventions,
Weigh discreetly their intentions,
  Thenceforth judge them white, or black.

Mark a poor and wandering nation
Saved from fangs of fell starvation,
  Harmless babes and mothers fed;
See it, when by foes unnumbered
Sore beset, and cooped and cumbered,
  Helped to raise its drooping head;

Mark the Seeress taught and aided,
Comforted when grief-invaded,
  Nerved to meet misfortune fell:
Deeds in light, not darkness, vested!
Trees are by their fruitage tested—
  Bore that tree the fruits of hell?

Think not that I fain would marry
Christian faith to faiths that tarry
  Cowering in the realms of night:
Wherefore mingle taper's gleaming,
Painfully, with glories streaming
  Broad upon the noonday bright?

Yet, mayhap, the gleam and glowing,
Hotly through the azure flowing,
  Fails to touch some tender shade,
Nestled where the waters brawling,
O'er a forest barrier falling,
  Many a caverned cleft have made.

There are found the timorous yellows,
Bashful greens, and red that fellows
Gently its companions pale;
There are found the emerald mosses,
Ferny fronds, and purple bosses—
Berries linked to leafage frail.

Bold the berries creep from under,
Lamb-like bold in simple wonder,
Vying with the flowerets gay;
Deeplier down the ferns are hidden,
Deeplier yet, like children chidden,
Hide the mosses from the day.

Surely one the cleft exploring,
Fain for wealth of Nature's storing,—
Grieved by darkness of the deeps,
Adverse to his eye's discerning
Balms to heal his bosom (yearning
Fondly o'er the love that sleeps

Fairest there where most in stillness
Holy fervour blends with chillness,
Power with things that smallest seem)—
Surely such one ne'er refuses
Shimmering radiance that diffuses
Sunlight through the falling stream?

Thus will loving hearts discover,
E'en where heathen clouds o'er-hover
Hauntingly a region wild,
Flowers most delicate in sweetness,
Desert plants of pure completeness
Imaging the angel-child;

Flowers to seek with footsteps tender,
Bruising not their faces slender,
Breathing not the airs of hate.
—Wouldst thou win the Mystic Flower,
Wisdom-giver, plant of power?
Love shall win it, soon or late.

Yea, the enchanter's work of magic,
Weirdly music, songs choragic,
Booming drums of sound obscure,—
These are but as mere excrescence,
Bloated body of an essence
Pure as heaven itself is pure.

Nought at most but means to settle,
Sure as lodestone fixes metal,
Feeble wish to forceful will;
Firm, unwavering concentration
Renders thought a far legation
Winged for realms of good, or ill.

Verily, a born magician
Spirits seek on many a mission,
  Nought by spell nor magic bound;
Drawn, by yearning sympathetic,
Him to haunt whose frame hermetic
  Makes a spectral meeting-ground.

Likewise knaves and triflers various
Reckless turn to games precarious
  Played with creatures of the gloom;
Close companioning with spirits
Earthliest moulded, by demerits
  Tethered to their corpses' tomb.

Yearnest thou for mystic power?
Never mayst thou win that dower
  Save when purged from earthly dross;
Stern and ruthless the purgation,
Wrought through fires of lone tentation,
  All things joyous held for loss.

Thus thou winnest might magnetic;
Openest thy sight prophetic,
  Closed while fleshly darkness reigns;
Drawest round thee through thy meetness
Spirit visitants of sweetness,
  Habitants of heavenly plains.

Few the prophets—few and hidden.
Shall the Meda be forbidden
  Rightful claim to prophet's meed?
Fasting, pureness, stress of trial,
Virtuous life beyond decrial,
  Many a high and noble deed,

All were hers,—and mystic vision
Witnessing with pure precision
  Things that are and things to be:
Rich her dowry transcendental,
Rich her moral dower and mental,—
  Truthful, wise, and prudent, she.

Through her being's consecration,
Stores of wondrous revelation
  Well she might have harvested;
Stores to feed our souls with beauty,
Nerving for the daily duty
  Hung about our hearts like lead.

Otherways the thing was fated.
She, whose wingèd soul had mated
  Soul of him on Patmos' shore,
Tamely clipped her eagle pinions,
Seared her spirit-eyes—as minions
  Torture birds that sing and soar.

Be it so. In modes essential
Doubtless seems her plan prudential:
  Exemplary was her life;
Peacefully she lived, respected;
Pleasantly by love protected,
  Won a third time as a wife.

Husband this of Christian habit,
James Wabôse (or, Snowy Rabbit),
  Nau-we-kwaish-kum once his name:
Heathen fancies long deserted,
Lived he as a man converted,
  Excellent beyond all blame.

Pleasantly in peaceful fashion,
Free from all perturbing passion,
  Dwelt this homely Christian pair;
Happy in their humble measure,
Sharing many a simple pleasure,
  Simple sorrows called to share;

Children given, and children taken,—
Little more to stir or waken
  Slumberous years that onward glide.
Furthermore the records show not;
How my heroine fared I know not,
  Know not how or when she died.

Doubtless through the realms of brightness
Walks she now in robes of whiteness,
  Radiant in celestial birth.
—Mid the dazzling maze of glory
Thinks she of the forests hoary,
  Plains and rivers of the earth?

Lapse of time, nor change of places,
Never from the soul effaces
  Lines on Memory's tablet scored.
Memory weights a demon's sorrow,
Memory makes an angel's morrow
  Bright with yesterdays restored.

NOTES.

NOTES.

Note 1.—*Winter Glories.*

Page 3.—'The shaggy cattle in the park.' This relates to the picturesque long-haired, wide-horned Highland breed. Pale reds or yellows, or grays varying from dun to silver-white, are very frequent colours, especially in lots chosen for a park.

Page 3.—'Crimson berries.' The fruit of that pretty creeper, the *Cotoneaster Microphylla.*

Note 2.—*Forest Fragrance.*

Page 6.—'O yellow Whin.' It may not be known to all readers that *Whin* is another name for Gorse or Furze.

Note 3.—*Sunset after Storm.*

Page 6.—Description of a sunset in Glen Clova; see Note 6.

Note 4.—*The Burial of Isis.*

Page 9.—This narrative (written in 1883) has no historical or traditional basis, nor does it pretend to strict antiquarian accuracy. The proper names are borrowed from old Celtic annals, but without reference to the persons recorded as bearing them.

Page 10.—'Alban' denoted northern Britain, till the name Scotia, or Scot-land, was transferred from Ireland to that country, after the subversion of Pictish by Scottish rule.

Page 11.—'Cruithnê' was a race-name, borne both by the Irish Picts and by the North Picts of Alban.

Pages 16, 21.—'Talurchan' and 'Urgust' (in varying forms) were the names of several Pictish dignitaries.

Page 16.—The 'Men of Strath-Clyde' belonged to the kingdom thus designated, which comprised Cumberland and the greater part of south-western Scotland. They were of Cymric race, not Gaels or Picts.

Page 19.—The 'Men of the East' may be taken to represent Picts, and the 'Men of the West' (page 17) to represent the Scots, a powerful Gaelic colony in Argyllshire, who were among the earlier converts to Christianity in those parts of the island.

Page 21.—'The shaveling priests.' These were the ecclesiastics sent from Rome to subvert the original Church in Alban. Their tonsure differed from that used by the native priests. These emissaries arrived at various times before the epoch of their final success; no particular date is meant to be fixed in the poem.

Page 15.—'Ainê,' or Ana, was a Lunar goddess worshipped in Erin and Alban as great Mother Nature, more or less corresponding to Kybelê or the Syrian Artemis

(Di-*ana*). Fountains, lakes, and rivers were generally, and often specially, sacred to this goddess.

Page 17.—'Cast the fateful rods' refers to a mode of divination said to have been practised by the Druids or other Celtic pagan priests.

Note 5.—*Complete and Incomplete.*

Page 24.—Written at Kissingen, in Bavaria, in 1877. The Argument consists in an attempt to show that on this earth perfection is only to be found in Nature's simpler works and in works of Art akin to these in spirit; while imperfection attaches to other works of Nature or Art, which belong to states of development, being fitted or destined for a higher ultimate perfection.

Page 35.—'Dwells in Melencolia's face. 'Melencolia' (thus spelt) is the inscription on a scroll, borne through the air by a bat-like dragon, in Albert Dürer's magnificent engraving, which represents a stately and mysteriously meditative woman seated amidst a chaos of incongruous objects.

Note 6.—*The Wanderer of Clova.*

Page 38.—A true story; the events described took place in 1859. The valley of Clova lies in the far north-west of Forfarshire,—a grand, but sombre and rather narrow glen, confined by steep mountains of great height, and traversed by the river South Esk, there first called by that name. At its upper end this valley forks into the wild rocky glens of Dole and Bachnagairn, down which flow the White Water and the Esk (here probably abbreviated from Eskendhui or Black Water—see old maps), the two head-streams of the river referred to. 'Tom-bũiê' is a dome-shaped mountain, over 3000 feet high, near the top of the upper part of Glen Dole; the name (entirely appropriate, like all Gaelic place-names) signifies the Yellow Rounded Hill.

NOTE 7.—*The Rocky Mountains.*

Page 47.—These verses relate to the mountain regions at the sources of the Athabasca and the two Saskâtchewans, visited by the Author in 1859.* The 'Siffleur,' or Whistler, is the small animal known to Naturalists as *Arctomys Pruinosus,* the Hoary Marmot. Its wildly plaintive music has a singular charm when heard amidst the stillness of the vast rock-solitudes.

NOTE 8.—*February in the Pyrenees.*

Page 50.—Written in 1883, while walking in the beautiful valley of Asté, near Bagnères de Bigorre.

NOTE 9.—*The German Tower Keeper.*

Page 57.--Generally descriptive of the Margarethen Tower at Gotha, visited by the Author in 1874.

* See *Saskatchewan* (Edinburgh, 1876), where will be found full descriptions of the Siffleur and other animals mentioned in the poem.

NOTE 10.—*Idle Talk.*

Page 61.—Alliterative, on the plan of some of the old Saxon poems.

NOTE 11.—*The Mountain Fir.*

Page 66.—The scene is laid in the Aberdeenshire forest of Glen Tanar, on the eastern side of the wooded glen of the Allachie, a little above Altnafearn.

NOTE 12.—*Golden Pigeons.*

Page 77.—Wood-pigeons, flying opposite the morning sun, will often reflect its rays and shine with the keen yellow lustre of burnished gold.

NOTE 13.—*Firs and Foxgloves.*

Page 81.—The scenery is that of the lower part of the Allachie, in Glen Tanar.

NOTE 14.—*Strength and Beauty.*

Page 99.—Generally descriptive of Craig Mellan in Glen Dole (Note 6).

NOTE 15.—*The Moorland Moth.*

Page 102.—*Bombyx Quercus* (otherwise termed *Bombyx Callunae*, or *Lasiocampa Roboris*); The Oak Egger. A large and lovely moth, of amber lights and russet shades, with a clear white spot on each of its upper wings.

Note 16.—*Coulen Forest.*

Page 108.—A rocky and partly wooded forest situated in western Ross-shire, where it once formed a portion of the vast Applecross territory. My verses were written in 1871. The Gaelic words are phonetically spelt.

Page 109.—'The Giant's grave.' A gigantic hero named Coulen is traditionally said to have been buried on an island in the stream connecting Loch Clair with the upper lake.

Note 17.—*Dea Incognita.*

Page 119.—An enthusiast beholding a beautiful unknown imagines her to be no mere mortal, but a vision of ideal Womanhood.

Page 120.—'Motherhood's ovoid of archetype light,' refers to the *kosmic egg* of early mythologies—the shape formed by the Creator, from æther, chaos, and night, to be the matrix of all things.

Note 18.—*The Sorrowful Varangian.*

Page 122.—The Varangians were Scandinavian rovers, who, after years of piratical enterprise, established a kingdom in north-western Russia, about the middle of the ninth century. Many of these adventurers passing, from time to time, into Greece, the Byzantine emperors formed from their number a bodyguard, which, constantly recruited from the North, remained for generations a mainstay of the imperial throne.—(Gibbon, *Decline and Fall*; Scott, *Count Robert of Paris.*) In the poem, one of these barbarous pagans, or semi-pagans, laments the loss of his Grecian mistress, raises a mound to her memory, and vows to immolate there the enemies who had caused her death.

NOTE 19.—*The Pine Marten.*

Page 124.—Pine Martens—handsome animals, of the Sable tribe—were not uncommon in Glen Tanar a few years ago. The Author has occasionally seen them playing among the trees in the remoter depths of the forest.

NOTE 20.—*The Eagle.*

Page 126.—'Dark Corrie Fee,' still, or recently, the haunt of wild goats and eagles, is a great semicircular recess bounded by ramparts of rock, situated amidst the mountains that overlook Glen Dole, in Clova (Note 6). The name is phonetically spelt 'Fee,' the true Gaelic form being unknown.

NOTE 21.—*The Flitch of Dunmow.*

Page 142.—Under an old custom at Dunmow, in Essex, a flitch of bacon is publicly given to any wedded pair who will make oath that they have dwelt together without shadow of discord for the twelve months succeeding their marriage. In the present song, a husband and wife, thus qualified, are supposed to be riding in procession to claim their reward.

Note 22.—*Rhyme and Reason.*

Page 167.—These verses were written in 1879, as a rejoinder to criticisms on certain rhymes used by the Author in his former publications. No personal disrespect, it need hardly be said, was, or is, meant towards the two distinguished poets (one lately deceased) some of whose less happy rhymes and phrases are reproduced or travestied.

Note 23.—*Frankie.*

Page 181.—The details of this true story are taken from a small book, by Miss Davies, entitled *The Helping Hand: or Stories of the Combe Boys' Home*, Dublin, 1875. My verses were published in 1877.

Note 24.—*The Chosen Casket.*

This poem was written under somewhat remarkable circumstances. Having experimented in what certain persons term 'Spirit-writing'—that is, letting the pen run on without conscious guidance,—and (after some practice) finding no difficulty as regarded prose, it one day occurred to me to try if verse could be produced in the same manner. Taking pen in hand, to my surprise thirty-two double-rhymed quatrains reeled themselves off (as it were) in less than as many minutes, and this notwithstanding two interruptions from persons entering the room to talk on everyday matters—which I was as well able to attend to as at any other time. These verses—almost blameless in rhyme and rhythm—were on strange and mystical subjects, most of them quite foreign to my usual thoughts.

Repeating the experiment on other occasions, I wrote several similar pieces under similar conditions,—some of them requiring more or less of subsequent correction in form. At length I invited my hand (so to speak) to write a narrative, instead of mystical disquisitions. The result was 'The Chosen Casket,' which was written thus—thirty-one verses in two hours, in the morning (March 16th, 1876); twenty-one, in about the same time, in the evening; and the remaining twelve verses on the following day. In all truth I can declare that, beyond the occasional anticipation of a line, my mind took no cognisance of the work that proceeded from my hand. Often there was a pause (as if for thought, but quite apart from mine,—a long pause before the title was dictated), sometimes even corrections of lines already written (to which my hand was guided by slight impulses impossible to describe), but no terms can be too strong in declaring the utter separation of this work from any ideas of my own—before, or then, or afterwards,—or in asserting the complete difference in mode of composition, both as to mental processes and rapidity of execution, between such pieces and those that are produced in an ordinary manner.

In revising the poem for its present place, I have not hesitated to alter a word here and there; but the total number of these amendments is very small, and they are so unimportant (a few changes of adjectives, conjunctions, etc.) that it seemed needless to specify them, especially as the original manuscript exists. In the 'Meda Maiden' volume, the poem called 'A Song of Cheer' (now reprinted) was written in the same manner (also 'Aspiration,' though only partially, for some of the lines were confused); as likewise 'Roses and Melodies,' which I have not reprinted, finding it rather vague and meaningless.

Regarding the nature and origin of these productions I offer no opinion, my mind being in uncertainty on the subject. I may, however, remark that in such works similarity of style and diction to those characteristic of their ostensible author proves nothing against the 'Spirit' theory, the writer being looked on as an instrument, like an organ or a flute, which cannot but discourse with its own voice and within its own compass, let who will dictate and impart the music.

Page 218.—'The mystery that links proud manhood and the purple woods.' Probably allusive to secrets embodied in the Dionysiac Mysteries. The words were first written 'purple *vines*,' and rhymed to 'twines,' but were presently changed to 'purple *woods*' and rhymed to 'broods,' the form given in the text.

Page 219.—'The vast celestial bird.' The Simoorg, or Roc, a conception belonging to all the Eastern mystical systems.

NOTE 25.—*In Memory of G. H. D.*

Page 241.—These sonnets refer to the lamented death of my friend George Hawkins Dempster, of Dun nichen.

NOTE 26.—*Greenwood's Farewell.*

Page 245.—The scene of the eagle attacking the deer (page 275) was beheld in Glen Tanar forest, some eighteen years ago, by the Author's late brother, the Honourable John Carnegie, R.N., and by the Head-stalker, John Milne—now, alas! also dead, prematurely cut off by a melancholy accident.

NOTE 27.—*Ben Dixie.*

Page 289.—Glen Dola and the Lodge represent—in a general way—Glen Dole and Glen Clova, and Aucharn Cottage, at the junction of those glens (see Note 6). The garden (page 292) is a not unfaithful sketch of the little garden at Aucharn, as it appeared when known to the Author, as recently as 1879.

NOTE 28.—*Pigworm and Dixie.*

Page 297.—This composition is designed to take its place with 'Ben Dixie' and 'Greenwood's Farewell' in a dramatic series—or rather, association of dramatic pieces more or less similar in purpose and idea. Certain critics have objected to it as reprehensibly 'coarse.' Yet how many persons delight in Dickens's low-life pictures, admire the rougher passages in Mr. Browning's poems, and specially applaud the Laureate's *Northern* and *Southern Farmers*; and how few would rebuke those eminent writers for the dramatic rudeness so harshly denounced in the works of an unrecognised hand!

If it be said, 'The question is one of skilled workmanship rather than of morals,' I reply, 'Then judge my work by that general law, not by one enacted for the occasion.' Condemn it at your pleasure on technical or metrical grounds, but forbear to rail at it for its mere quality of coarseness, unless you can prove it to outdo in that respect the licence conceded elsewhere, or unless you are ready to condemn all coarseness, anywhere and everywhere—a perfectly defensible position.

Those who dislike the portraiture of low life are in no way bound to read 'Pigworm.' Those who do so will discover in it, I hope and believe, nothing worse than the mere blunt uncouthness of handling that the subject absolutely requires.

NOTE 29.—*The Anchorite.*

Page 310.—An altogether imaginary narrative. The redundant syllable in the third line of each stanza is purposely introduced.

Page 311.—'When naked Fulvia frantic stood.' Incantations were supposed to be more acceptable to the unseen powers when performed in a state of nudity.

Page 312.—'And scanned the marks her fingers tore.' The form of divination referred to was frequently practised in the days of the Cæsars. It consisted in slaying a boy or maiden, and reading mystic secrets in the marks convulsively scored on the ground by the dying victim.

Page 317.—'I see the emerald in his hand.' It is related that the Emperor Nero was accustomed to view the sports of the arena through, or in, an emerald, which relieved, or assisted, his defective sight. Probably this was nothing more than a lens formed from beryl or some other translucent stone of greenish hue.

Page 321.—'The upward, or the downward, thumb.' At the Roman games the audience decided the fate of a vanquished combatant, by lowering their thumbs as a death-warrant, or by raising them in the rare cases when mercy was shown to some exceptionally valiant man. The narrator, in the present story, being suspected by the Emperor of friendship for the assailed Christians, is malignantly commanded to guide him in pronouncing his award—all-powerful for pardon or for death.

NOTE 30.—*The Chamorra.*

Page 323.—This poem is founded on a story in Mr. Latouche's *Travels in Portugal,* the details of which have in most cases been carefully followed.

Page 324.—'Green wine of virtue rare.' A country wine, of the colour and qualities described.

Page 334.—'Chamorra.' A common Portuguese designation for one whose hair is closely cropped.

Page 349.—'Lobis-homem.' A were-wolf; that is, a human being who can at pleasure assume a wolf-form for purposes of rapine.

Page 354.—'Padrê Paul.' The description of this country priest, as to costume, taste in diet, peasant-like manners, etc., is fully warranted by Mr. Latouche's book.

Page 356.—'The Bruxas.' These are witches, who act as mentioned in the poem.

THE MEDA MAIDEN.

NOTE 31.—*Introductory Notes.*

(31*a*) Page 361.—*Introduction.* The story of the 'Meda Maiden' (the Seeress or Enchantress) is to be found in Mr. Schoolcraft's Report on the Indian Tribes of the United States, a national work, in five quarto volumes, published about thirty years ago 'Under the Act of Congress approved March 3d, 1847.'* In the official communication from the 'Secretary of the Interior,' where this *imprimatur* appears, cordial testimony is borne to the 'labour, learning and ability,' displayed by Mr. Schoolcraft in framing his Report, and his fitness for the task assigned to him may be further established by a quotation from his own remarks in the Introduction to the earlier portion of the book. He thus expresses himself:—'The author has devoted many years of his leisure to these investigations [viz. as to the history, languages, antiquities, and manners and cústoms, of the Indians]

* SCHOOLCRAFT (Henry R., LL.D.), *The Indian Tribes of the United States*, 4to, 5 vols., Philadelphia, 1851-6. Where not otherwise specified, the quoted passages throughout the Notes on 'The Meda Maiden' are taken from that work. While quoting with general accuracy, I have here and there made unimportant changes in spelling, arrangement of sentences, italicising, etc. The words in square brackets are always my own.

while residing in an official capacity in the West. . . . Thirty years thus spent on the frontiers, and in the forests, where the Red Race still dwells, have exhibited them to his observation in almost every possible development. . . . The peculiarly intimate relations the author has held to them (*having married a highly-educated lady, whose grandfather was a distinguished aboriginal chief-regnant or king*,) has had the effect of breaking down towards himself, individually, the eternal distrust of the Indian mind, and to open the most secret arcana of his hopes and fears.'

These circumstances considered, it would be hard to question Mr. Schoolcraft's competency in matters relating to the Indians, and there can be no reason to doubt or impugn his honesty and absolute good faith. He alludes to my heroine's general prophetic career, and recounts the experiences more specially before us, as if dealing with actual facts—true not merely in the Meda's own impressions, but true in themselves; and strange as the tale may seem, many people in America, and perhaps elsewhere, will find no difficulty in thinking it credible, and in admitting the claim of this Seeress to prophetic and magical powers. But, setting that aside, and dismissing as baseless fancies all visions and previsions, the story itself, nevertheless, seems to me to retain much value, as a characteristic record of the manners of a valiant, once formidable, and ever interesting race, and I therefore venture to hope for it some measure of approval, even from persons disinclined to accept or tolerate the spiritualism it so prominently brings forward.

To explain some parts of the poem that might be thought obscure, I have embodied in the present notes, not only such details as are obviously relevant, but likewise many particulars that seemed usefully illustrative of the religious beliefs and magical practices of the American Indians. For these purposes I have used Mr. Schoolcraft's Report as my chief source of information. Though so many years have elapsed since the issue of that work, I have preferred it for my special purposes to more recent publications; partly on account of its official character, partly because it necessarily records the opinions of the Indians at the period of a story which is taken from its pages,—opinions now perhaps modified (however slightly) by the advance of civilisation, and the influence of Christianity in various forms.

It will hardly escape the reader's notice that the scenes and localities of my poem are very similar to those treated of in Mr. Longfellow's 'Hiawatha,' while its story relates to the same tribe—the Ojibways, inhabitants of Minnesota, or of the adjacent districts in British Territory. This coincidence will not seem singular when it is remembered that the Indians now referred to have for years been in constant intercourse with their European neighbours, being among the nearest, most friendly, and most accessible of the wild, or half-wild, tribes, which retain a partial independence on the borders of civilisation. When 'The Meda Maiden' verses were written, long time had passed since I had even looked upon the pages of 'Hiawatha'—that truest and best of forest poems—full of lovely nature

—faultless in *keeping*—the work of one familiar with the land and the life he so admirably describes—and I borrowed nothing from it save the name of the Manito of death, and the general idea (but differently used) of the metrical cadence—one, indeed, of very ancient origin, —a cadence that strangely harmonises in its monotony with such feelings as are inspired and impressed by the immensity and calm persistence in sameness of vast forests and wide prairies, and smooth, deep-channelled, slowly moving rivers.

As the poem very closely follows Mr. Schoolcraft's narrative, it seems needless to quote from him at length regarding the 'Meda Maiden's' life and history; a few extracts, however, in reference to matters elsewhere omitted or but slightly touched on, may form a useful ending for these introductory notes.

(31*b*) Pages 361, 367, 393.—*Memoir of the Meda Maiden.* 'Chusco, a noted prophet of the Ottawas,' writes Mr. Schoolcraft, 'practised the prophet's art, for a great number of years, at his native village of L'Arbre Croche, on Lake Michigan, and also at Michillimackinac, where he died at an advanced age, in 1838. There also came to reside at the latter place, a prophetess [named Ogeewyahn Oqut Oqua] from Chegoimegan, on the shores of Lake Superior. [Born about 1802], she was a descendant in a direct line from one of the principal Ojibway families, [of which was] the noted Waubojeeg, the ruling chief in that quarter.'

Waubojeeg, as we elsewhere learn, was a celebrated

war-chief and ruler of his tribe, who died about 1793. He belonged to the family of the Addik or Reindeer, a distinguished Ojibway clan, who bore that animal for their *totem*, or armorial cognisance. His own name signifies 'White Fisher'—the Fisher being an animal of the Mink or Marten tribe. By blood, Waubojeeg was partly a Sioux, related to Wabashaw, chief of a band of that nation. His father, Mamongeseda, commanded the Ojibways, in alliance with the French, at the capture of Quebec in 1759; Waubojeeg, then a child, grew up to be a warm friend to the British. The 'grave-board' of Waubojeeg records that he headed no less than seven war-parties, and received three serious wounds. On a comparison of dates, he might well have been grandfather to the 'Meda Maiden.' In recent times there have been two other distinguished warriors of the same name and tribe:—Waubojeeg, slain by the Sioux, shortly before 1800; and Waubojeeg, spoken of as '*now* [about 1850] a noted chief of the Mississippi bands, fully sustaining the name of his . . . two illustrious namesakes.' (See Sch. i. 356, 390; ii. 143, 163; v. 524.)

'It was the same fact [conversion to Christianity] as that which had brought Chusco within the pale of inquiry, that also revealed the gods [*i.e. manitoes* or spirits] of Ogeewyahn Oqut Oqua, or the prophetess of Chegoimegan.* She had felt and acknowledged the truth of

* Otherwise given as *Ogeewyahnoquot Okwa*, or *Ogeewyahn ackwut oquay*. Mr. Schoolcraft constantly varies the spelling of Indian words. In some cases the pronunciation is given, in others left uncertain. The meaning of the prophetess's name is

the exhortations of one of the native preachers from the shores of Lake Ontario, in Canada, the noted John Sunday, and had united herself tò a missionary [Methodist] church. At this period she was baptized, and subsequently married to an Indian convert, called Wabôse, or the Hare [more commonly, Rabbit], on which occasion she relinquished her former name, and assumed that of Wabôse. . . . Catherine Wabôse was still living at the last accounts [when she was 'in her forty-first year'—Sch. i. 395—not earlier seemingly than 1843]. She is a female of good natural intellect, great shrewdness of observation, and some powers of induction and forecast. . . . In order to understand the force and character of her delineations [symbolical drawings, termed *kekeenowin*,—see Note 40], it was deemed important to obtain the history of the operations of her mind under the influence of her primary periodical fast. *This she related in the Indian tongue to Mrs. Schoolcraft, who took it down from her lips.*'

Then follows the story adopted in the present poem, and related with strict adherence to the details of the nar-

not stated. *Oqut* or *Ackwut* signifies a Cloud, *Ogeewyahn* is some epithet characterising *Oqut*, and *Oqua* seems to be merely the feminine designation (Ang. *Squaw*), a Woman ; thus the whole would signify—*The woman of the . . . cloud.* 'Names are generally bestowed by the . . . matron, or aged grandmother of the family, who generally connects the event with some dream. If the child be a male, the name is generally taken from some object in the visible heavens . . . such as—*Returning Cloud, Bright Sky.* . . . If it be a female, the imagery is generally drawn from the surface of the earth. . . . *Woman of the passing stream, Woman of the green valley, Woman of the rock,* are not uncommon names.' —(Sch. ii. 65, 66.)

rative. Regarding this, says Mr. Schoolcraft in conclusion:—'These particulars, it is conceived, will afford *a clear and satisfactory chain of evidence of the truth of her* [*Ogeewyahn Oqut Oqua's*] *narrative*, and the reason why she has been willing to impart secrets of her past life which have heretofore been studiously concealed, as she remarks, even from her nearest friends.'—(Schoolcraft, i. 390-397.)

NOTE 32.—*General Notes.*

(32*a*) Page 374.—'The Woman that liveth for Ever.' *Kau-ge-gay-be-qua*, the Everlasting Woman, or Everlasting Standing Woman.

(32*b*) Page 374.—'Mônido-Wininees.' The Little Man-spirit, or Little Spirit-man.

(32*c*) Page 375.—'A wide door in the firmament riven.' 'An orifice in the heavens, called *Pug-un-ai-au-geezhik.*'

(32*d*) Page 375.—'The firmament's portal.' The firmament—*O-Shau-wau-e-geezhik*, the Blue Sky, or Bright Blue Sky.

(32*e*) Page 378.—'Ruddy head of bird.' The Red-headed Woodpecker.

(32*f*) Page 385.—'Strong-Sky.' *O-mush-kow-egeezhik.* In the lines immediately preceding, the expression, 'Yields to music soft and tender,' partly refers to a mode of courtship common among the Indian tribes, and probably practised by the Ojibways, in which the young lover intimates his feelings by daily stationing himself near the chosen maiden's dwelling and playing on a musical instrument like a flute.

(32*g*) Page 395.—'Fair-Cloud.' *Minan-oqut.*

(32*h*) Page 395.—'Pauguk.' The Manito of death.

(32*i*) Page 396.—'The Snowy Owl.' A magnificent bird of prey; as large in body as some of the eagles, though shorter of wing.

(32*j*) Page 397.—'Rest in the ancestral grave.' The Indians attach much importance to an honourable burial; see Note 34, p. 458.

(32*k*) Page 405.—'Hasted to the Happy Land.' Regarding the dream of the Meda-woman's son, Mr. Schoolcraft's words are as follows:—'Her son, by Strong-Sky, sickened at an age when he began to be useful, and after lingering for a time, died. A day or two before his departure, he related to her such a dream of the Great Spirit, as he is known and worshipped by the Whites, and of his being clothed by Him with a white garment, that her mind was much affected by it, and led to question, in some measure, the soundness of her religious views.' Nothing further is said on the subject of this vision, but in my poem I have fitted to it some of the details of an Iroquois story to be found in the same volume, entitled 'The Island of the Blessed, or the Hunter's Dream.'—(Sch. i. 321.)

(32*l*) Page 409.—'Grand Ojibway name.' Though the Ojibway names may look strange in English spelling, the language is not without dignity, as spoken. Howse, in his *Cree Grammar*, comparing it with other Indian tongues, terms it the 'sonorous, majestic Chippeway [Ojibway].' On this subject see my *Saskatchewan*, p. 287. 'John Sunday's' Ojibway appellation is not given by Mr. Schoolcraft; he seems to have been a well-known 'evangelist,' or missionary teacher.

(32*m*) Page 413.—'The garb of rare devices, snowy-white.' Such garments are made from the dressed skins of the Bison or of the Mountain Sheep, laboriously brought to extreme softness, pipe-clayed, and painted with devices in various colours. Ornamentally beaded tunics of leather thus prepared are commonly worn by women, but robes highly decorated with paint belong rather to male than to female attire; the Meda-woman, however, in her character as seeress occupied an exceptional place, and her dress may well have been peculiar and conspicuous, at all events on official occasions.

(32*n*) Page 416.—'Him that finished what good "Sunday" had begun.' This refers to Mr. Schoolcraft, who appears to have interested himself in the Meda-woman's further progress in Christianity. One of the seeress's daughters, by Strong-Sky, was 'educated and instructed under the personal care of Mrs. Schoolcraft, who cherished her as a tender plant from the wilderness.'

NOTE 33.—*Indian Fasts.*

Page 363.—'The initial Fast at the age of puberty which every Indian undergoes, is for light to . . . become aware of his personal Manito [Spirit]. When revealed in dreams, his purpose is accomplished, and he adopts that revelation, which is generally some bird or animal, as his personal or guardian Manito. He trusts in it in war and peace; and there is no exigency in life in which he believes it cannot help him.'—(Sch. i. 34.)

'To prepare a candidate for admission to the Society of the Meda, his chief reliance for success is upon his early dreams and fasts. If these bode good, he is inclined to persevere in his preparations, and to make known to the leading men of the institution, from time to time, the results.'—(Sch. i. 360.)

'Chingwauk [an Ojibway chief, a Christian, "previously one of the most noted professors of the Medawin"] began by saying that the ancient Indians made a great merit of fasting. They fasted sometimes six or seven days, till both their bodies and minds became free and light, which prepared them to dream. The object of the ancient seers was to dream of the sun, as it was believed that such a dream would enable them to see everything on the earth. And by fasting long, and thinking much on the subject, they generally succeeded. Fasts and dreams were first attempted at an early age. What a young man sees and experiences during these dreams and fasts, is adopted by him as truth, and it becomes a principle to regulate his future life. . . . If he has been much favoured in his fasts, and the people believe that he has the art of looking into futurity, the path is open to the highest honours.'—(Sch. i. 113, 114.)

Note 34.—*Religion of the Indians.*

Page 366.—'The American Indians worship with more truth and purity [than most nations holding similar beliefs] the being of a universal God, or *Mánito*, who is called in the North, the Great, Good, or Merciful Spirit—or *Gezha Manito.* This Great Spirit is believed to rule the earth and the sky, and to be the *Wa-zha-waud*, or maker of the world—the original animating Principle. To his power they oppose an antagonistical Great Evil-minded Spirit—*Matchi Manito* (symbolised often by the serpent)—who is constantly seeking to destroy and overturn all good and benevolent measures.

'There is no attempt . . . which can be gathered from their oral traditions, to impute to the Great Merciful Spirit the attribute of justice, or to make man accountable to Him, here or hereafter, for aberrations from virtue, good-will, truth, or any form of moral right.' [Yet see the Iroquois story called 'The Island of the Blessed,'—whence I have adapted the dream of the Meda-woman's dying son,—where the Master of Life permits two persons to pass safely into Paradise, because 'the thoughts and acts of neither of them had been bad.'—(Sch. i. 322.) This tale is perhaps modified by European notions.] 'With benevolence and pity as prime attributes, the Great Transcendental Spirit of the Indian does not take upon himself a righteous administration of the world's affairs, but on the contrary leaves it to be filled, and its affairs *in reality* governed by demons. . . . There are malignant as well as benevolent Manitoes. The Great Spirit leaves these two antagonistical classes to war with each other, and to counteract each other's designs, to fill the world with turmoils, and in fact to govern the *moral* destinies of mankind.'—(Sch. i. 34, 35, 38.)

It seems uncertain whether the Gezha Manito and the Matchi Manito are to be deemed equals in power and greatness, or whether (as rather appears) the former holds a distinct place of all-supreme sovereignty, while the Great Bad Spirit is but a subordinate though potential being, who presides over the minor spirits of evil, for ever warring against the minor spirits of good. Unquestionably the Great Good Spirit is regarded with more respect than his opponent, and is alone styled *Wazhawaud*, or Creator; but it is to the Evil Power that offerings are chiefly given and acts of homage paid. The Iroquois 'suppose, at the creation, the birth of *two antagonistical powers* of miraculous energy, but *subordinate to the Great Spirit*' (Sch. i. 32); it is not stated whether the Ojibways and other Algonquin tribes accept the same belief.

'In common with the best of the plain Indians,' writes Colonel Dodge, 'the Cheyennes [of the Dacota race, like their neighbours the Sioux] believe in two gods, equals in wisdom and power. One is the *good god* . . . from him come all the pleasurable things of life. . . . The other is the *bad god* . . . from him come all pain, suffering, and disaster.'—(Dodge, *The Hunting Grounds of the Great West*, 1877, p. 272.)

Subordinate to the two great Manitoes there is a vast

assemblage of spirits peopling all nature; these beings are likewise entitled *Mánito* (or *Mónedo*) by the Algonquin tribes, and all the American Indians have some equivalent designation. The term simply signifies 'a spiritual or mysterious power,' when not modified by a 'prefix or accent.'

To every individual (it would seem) is assigned a special Manito, or guardian spirit, and the 'initial fast at the age of puberty, which every Indian undergoes, is for light to be individually advertised of, and become aware of, this personal Manito.'—(Sch. i. 34.) A 'strong' Manito is a desideratum, for 'the Manitoes are not of equal or harmonious power, . . . hence the Indian is never sure that his neighbour is not under the guardianship of a Manito stronger than his own. The doctrine that a man may possess such a power [mystic might, through communion with spirits] is well established in the belief of all the tribes. All their priests and prophets assert the possession of it. . . . A man may fast to obtain this mysterious power.'—(Sch. i. 34.)

The Indians are also 'worshippers of the elements, of fire, and the sun; and hymns and offerings are made to the latter.'—(Sch. i. 38.)

'The mythology of the Ojibways is one which creates a frequent necessity of speaking of spiritual and immaterial existences, which are supposed to inhabit the sky and the air, and which are invested by them with the powers of *ubiquity* and *immateriality*. Although these creations are thought to be often manifest to the eye, and are typified in clouds, rainbows, lightnings, thunder, and a thousand varying phenomena on the earth connected with the exhibition of light and shade, they are also clothed with the power of *invisibility*. Their materiality as phenomena of the heavens is changed in a moment to spirituality.

'The Indian mythology could not exist without this theory. The Great Spirit is supposed to inhabit the heavens, and to walk "on the wings of the wind." Nobody can hear an Indian Meda, Prophet, or Jossakeed speak on the great phenomena around him, without perceiving this. And the impression of his notions of spiritual existence becomes absolute when we see him kneel down and lift up his voice in prayer. "*Nosa gebigong abeyun showainimegoyun*—My Father in heaven dwelling, take pity on us." This is not addressed to the father of a lodge, but to the Father of Light.'—(Sch. ii. 435.)

'They believe in the general doctrine of the metempsychosis, or transmigration of souls. . . . The soul of man is thought to be immortal, the vital spark passing from one object to another. This object of the new life in general is *not* man, but some species of the animated creation; or even, it may be, for a time, an inanimate object. The circumstances which determine this change do not appear.'—(Sch. i. 33.)

Yet some of the tribes would seem to hold a nobler creed. 'The idea of immortality is strongly dwelt upon. It is not spoken of as a supposition or a mere belief, not fixed. It is regarded as an actuality. . . . The resignation, nay, the alacrity, with which an Indian frequently lies down and surrenders life, is to be ascribed to this prevalent belief. He does not fear to go to a land which, all his life long, he has heard abounds in rewards without punishments.' . . . 'I was present with an interpreter,' continues Mr. Schoolcraft, 'in Upper Michigan, in 1822, when the interment of a warrior and hunter [doubtless an Ojibway] took place, at which the corpse was carefully dressed, and after it was brought to the grave, and before the lid was nailed to the coffin, an address was made by an Indian to the corpse. The substance of it relating to this belief was this:—"You are about to go to that land where our forefathers have gone—you have finished your journey here, before us. We shall follow you, and rejoin the happy groups which you will meet." When the speaking and ceremonies were concluded, the coffin was lowered into the trench prepared to receive it. This mode of interment is common to the forest tribes of the north, and appears to have been practised from the earliest periods. They choose dry and elevated places for burial.' —(Sch. ii. 68, 69.)

'It has been found that they believe in the *duality of the soul*. This ancient doctrine is plainly announced as existing among the Algonquins . . . who, believing i this duality, and that the soul sensorial abides for a time with the body in the grave, requiring food for its ghostly existence and journeyings, deposit meats and other aliment, at and after the time of interment. This custom is universal, and was one of their earliest observed traits.' (Sch. i. 33, 38, 39.)

'Another custom near akin to it prevails. They offer pieces of flesh and viands at meals and feasts, to their *O-git-te-zeem-e-wug*, or ancestors. This duty seems to be obligatory on every Indian in good standing with his tribe, who has been, so to say, piously instructed by the Medas or his parents; and the consequence is, he fears to neglect it. . . . The first idea that a grave, or burial-ground, or *ad-je-dá-tig* (grave-post) suggests to him, is the duty he owes as an honest man, expecting good luck in life, to his relatives, or *Ogittezeemewug*.'—(Sch. i. 39.)

According to recent accounts, similar beliefs are prevalent among the tribes of the Dacota race.

The Cheyenne or Sioux holds that—'all persons of all sexes, ages, colours, or beliefs, who died unscalped or unstrangled, will meet in the Happy Hunting Grounds—that final home of bliss. He goes there just as he was here, with the same passions, feelings, wishes, and needs. His favourite pony is killed at his burying-place, to enjoy an eternity of beautiful pasture, and to bear his master in war or in the chase. He will need arms to defend himself against enemies (man or beast): his rifle, pistol, bow, and quiver are buried with him. . . . All things which the Indian can make for himself in this life he can make in the next, . . . but articles beyond his skill in manufacture—gun, powder, lead, caps, etc.—must all be carried into the next world by the dead man. . . . He understands perfectly well that the dead does not actually take with him into the next world the material articles buried with him in this . . . he believes, however, that if the articles are allowed to remain with or near the body until decomposition is completed, the dead man will have in the next world the use of the phantoms of those articles. . . . Any article supposed necessary in a future state which the dead man did not possess in life, is at once supplied by relatives and friends, often at considerable sacrifice.'—(Dodge, *The Hunting Grounds*, pp. 283-285.)

'The Indians believe in spirits, also that if they do not live up to the laws or customs of their forefathers, the spirits will punish them for their misconduct, particularly if they omit to make feasts for the dead. They suppose these spirits have power to send the spirit of some animal to enter their bodies, and make them sick.'—(Sch. ii. 199.)

It is not clear to me whether (like modern spiritualists) the Indian Magician ever professes to converse with the spirits of the dead, or whether his mystic communion is solely with the elemental Manitoes already spoken of, who would seem to be beings of an entirely distinct nature. Save in exceptional cases, Indian beliefs are hard to ascertain. 'The Indian is not a man prone to describe his god [Manito], personal or general, but he is ready to depict him by a symbol.. He may conceal under the figure of a serpent, a turtle, or a wolf,—wisdom, strength, or malignity; or convey under the picture of a sun the idea of a Supreme All-seeing Intelligence. But he is not prepared to discourse on these things. What he believes on this head he will not declare to a White Man or a stranger. His happiness and success in life are thought to depend upon the secrecy of that knowledge of the Creator and his system, in the Indian view of benign and malignant agents. To reveal this to others, even to his own people, is, he believes, to expose himself to the counteracting influence of other agents known to his subtle scheme of necromancy and superstition, and to hazard success and life itself.'—(Sch. i. 340.)

The Meda woman could have offered no stronger proof of sincere conversion to Christianity than in revealing the mysteries of her native magic, which she had learnt to deem so valuable while hidden, so terrible and dangerous if sacrilegiously betrayed.

NOTE 35.—*Medâwin and Jeesukâwin.*

Page 379.—'There are two institutions among the North American Indians, which will be found to pervade the whole body of the tribes from the Atlantic to the Pacific, and from the Gulf of Mexico to the Arctic Ocean. . . . They are called [in Ojibway] the Medâwin and the Jeesukâwin—the *Art of Medical Magic*, and the *Art of Prophecy*.... Both are very ancient in their origin.'

MEDAWIN.—'The Meda, or Meda-wininee, is in all respects a [priestly] magician.* He is distinct from the

* *Meda* is a verb, according to Mr. Schoolcraft; nevertheless he and other writers in the same collection generally use it also as a noun. *Meda-wininee* is the word that literally signifies Meda-man.

Muskêkê-wininee, or medical practitioner, who administers medicines, bleeds, etc. The latter takes his denomination from *mus-kê-kê*, a liquid dose: the former from *meda*, a mysterious principle. The one is a physician, the other a priest. . . . Attempts of the Medas to heal the sick are only made when the patients have been given over by the Muskêkê-wininee. To *meda* is to perform magic, to trick by magic. *Medawin* is the art of magic. Men who profess this art are formed into societies. They are admitted by a public ceremony, after having been instructed in private, and given evidence of their skill and fitness. There is no order of descent. The thing is perfectly voluntary. Any one may become a follower and practiser of the *meda*. All that is necessary is to produce proofs of his skill.' . . . 'His chief reliance for success is upon his early dreams and fasts.'—(Sch. i. 358-360.)

'There is a modification of the Medawin, . . . it is the Wâbeno . . . of modern origin . . . a degraded form of the mysteries of the Meda. . . . The term is a derivative from *Wabun*, the morning light. Its orgies are protracted till morning dawn . . . if the sound of the Indian drum be heard after midnight, it may generally be inferred with certainty to proceed from the circle of the Wabenoes. . . . It permits the introduction of a class of subjects which are studiously excluded from the Meda. . . . Songs of love mingle in its mysteries . . . and deceptions . . . which derive their effect from the presence of darkness.'—(Sch. i. 366.)

JEESUKAWIN.—'The art of prophecy, or the Jeesukâwin,

differs from the Medâwin, in its being practised alone by distinct and solitary individuals, who have no associates. . . . Prophets start up at long intervals, and far apart, among the Indian tribes. They profess to be under supernatural power, and to be filled with a divine afflatus. It is, however, an art resembling that of the Medawin . . . differing chiefly in the object sought. The Meda seeks to propitiate events, the Jossakeed [prophet] aims to predict them. Both appeal to spirits for their power. Both exhibit material substances, as stuffed birds, bones, etc., as objects by or through which the secret energy is to be exercised. The general modes of operation are similar, but vary. The drum is used in both, but the songs and incantations differ. The rattle is confined to the ceremonies of the Meda and the Wabeno.

'The Jossakeed addresses himself exclusively to the Great Spirit . . . (which may equally mean the Great Good, or the Great Bad Spirit. The latter must as a general rule be inferred, where the term *Gezha* is not prefixed.)* The Jossakeed's office and his mode of address are regarded with greater solemnity and awe. His choruses are peculiar, and are deemed by the people to carry an air of higher reverence and devotion.'—(Sch. i. 359.) 'There is no art of higher pretensions to supernatural or divine power, among the professors of the Indian mysteries, than those which are made in the exhibitions of the sacred Jeesukawin. . . . To *jeesuka* (in the language of the Ojibways) is to mutter . . . the

* Over-stated: *e.g.* see *ante*, p. 456; or Tanner's *Narrative of Thirty Years among the* [*Ojibway*] *Indians* (1830), p. 46.

word is taken from the utterance of sounds of the human voice, low on the ground—the position in which the response is made by the seër or prophet, who is called *jossakeed.* [Jeesukâ, to prophesy—Jeesukâ-win, prophecy—Jeesuka-un (*a-un* pro. *aun*), a prophet's lodge—Jossakeed (by permutation from Jessuka-d), a prophet or seer; sometimes Jessuka-wininee, prophecy-man.'—(Sch. i. 388, 389.)]

'The whole tendency of the Indian secret institutions is to acquire power, through belief in a multiplicity of spirits; to pry into futurity by this means, that he may provide against untoward events [Jeesukawin]; to propitiate the class of benign spirits, that he may have success in war, in hunting, and in the medical art [Medawin]; or by acceptable sacrifices, incantations, and songs to the class of malignant spirits, that his social intercourse and passions may have free scope [Wabeno].'—(Sch. i. 368.)

Reporting on the Winnebagoes, a Dacota tribe who were settled near the Wisconsin river, Mr. Fletcher, the United States agent, thus expresses himself (in Mr. Schoolcraft's book) in reference to their magical observances:—'Whether these medicine-men [Medas] possess the secret of mesmerism or magnetic influence, or whether the whole system is a humbug and imposition, is difficult to determine. A careful examination of the ceremonies of this order for six years has been unable to detect the imposition, if there be one; and it is unreasonable to suppose that an imposition of this character could be practised for centuries without detection.'—(Sch. iii. 288.)

Note 36.—*The Ojibways.*

Page 379.—The Indian tribes inhabiting those countries between the Atlantic and the Rocky Mountains, which extend along the boundary between British America and the United States, are members of one or other of three great races, dissimilar in language, however alike in various respects,—viz. the Iroquois, the Dacôtas, and the Algonquins.

The Iroquois, now much diminished in number, and mostly half-civilised, occupied or occupy Western New York and the shores of Lakes Erie, Huron, and Ontario. To them belonged the confederated Six Nations so celebrated in history—the Mohawks, Oneidas, Onondagas, Cayugas, Senecas, and Tuscaroras, as well as other less conspicuous tribes.

The Dacôtas comprise the Sioux, and their off-shoot the Assiniboines, also the Pawnees, Mandans (extinct?), and other tribes,—nearly all dwellers on the prairie, and for the most part within the confines of the United States.

To the Algonquin race belonged the old Lenni Lenapi or Delaware nation. Its most prominent present members are the Ojibways, of the eastern forests; the Crees, of the northerly central plains; likewise the partly distinct Blackfeet or Satsikas, living in the country that borders with the mountains of the far West; of these the Crees alone entirely inhabit British territory.

The Ojibways (Odjibwas, or Ojibbeways), a very valiant and once powerful tribe, are settled on both sides of the international boundary. When first discovered by the French, more than two centuries ago, they were dwelling on the southern shore of Lake Superior,—an island named Moningwunakaun, now Lapointe, forming then their chief settlement. 'They have passed westward,' says their historian, 'till they occupy all the country about the headwaters of the Mississippi, and stand one foot on the edge of the vast western prairies, and the other on the dense forests of Eastern America' (Sch. ii. 137)—a description still sufficiently correct.

At the time of my American journey (1859), a considerable number inhabited the northern part of Minnesota, in the States. In British territory they occupied the country between Lake Superior and Red River, and extended westward up the Assiniboine and Qu'Appelle rivers till they came in contact with the plain-dwelling Crees, akin in blood and language, though now entirely distinct. Under many heroic chiefs the Ojibways have for generations waged war with their implacable enemies the Sioux—the leading nation of the Dacotas—overcoming them in many a desperate fight, and steadily driving them westward; then occupying their country, till European interference debarred further progress.

The Ojibways are often written of as *Chippeways*, but this name is inaccurate, besides inconveniently resembling that of the Chippeweyans, a very dissimilar race, who inhabit the remoter northern regions lying eastward from the Rocky Mountains.

As a rule, the Ojibways—pedestrians of the forest—

are less picturesque in aspect than the Crees and other wild horsemen of the plains, their dress being chiefly composed of cloth and blanketing, instead of the far handsomer leathern materials still in use among the tribes less immediately in contact with Europeans; but they yield to no native race in valour and the other distinguishing virtues of the American Indian, and in their general character appear to excel most of their uncivilised brethren.

Note 37.—*Meda Lodge.*

Page 381.—'To prepare the operator in the Meda mysteries for answering questions, a lodge is erected by driving stout poles, or saplings, in a circle, and swathing them round tightly from the ground to the top with skins, drawing the poles closer at each turn or wind, so that the structure represents a rather acute pyramid. The number of poles is prescribed by the Jossakeed [or Meda], and the kind of wood. There are sometimes, perhaps generally, ten poles, each of a different kind of wood. When this structure has been finished, the operator crawls in, by forcing his way under the skin at the ground, taking with him his drum, and scarcely anything beside. He begins his supplications by kneeling, and bending his body very low, so as almost to touch the ground. When his incantations and songs have been continued the requisite time, and he professes to have called around him the spirits (or Manitoes) upon whom he relies, he announces to the assembled multitude without, his readiness to give responses.'—(Sch. i. 389.)

'To exhibit the power of the operator, or officiating priest, in the Curative Art, an elongated lodge is expressly erected from poles and foliage newly cut, and particularly prepared for this purpose. This work is done by assistants of the Society, who obey specific directions, but are careful to exclude such species of wood or shrubbery as may be deemed detrimental to the patient.'—(Sch. i. 360.)

NOTE 38.—*Meda Drum.*

Page 381.—In all their magical ceremonies the Indians make use of the Drum (*Ta-wa-e-gun*, in the Ojibway language), and in those of the Wabeno they also employ the rattle. The object is the same—to call the attention of the invoked Manitoes or spirits, who, like ordinary corporeal beings, are supposed to require an audible summons. See, for example, the eighteenth hieroglyph of a Wabeno song, as described by Mr. Schoolcraft (Sch. i. 368-373): —'A young man, under the control of love, with feathers on his head, and a drum and drumstick in his hands. He affects power to influence the object of his desires—"Hear my drum—hear my drum, though you be on the other side of the earth, hear my drum."'

Many other barbarous or half-barbarous races made, or still make, similar use of the magic drum. The Laplanders moreover developed it into an instrument of divination, by painting numbers of figures on its parchment head, over which a small bone or metal object danced at the vibration of each stroke from the officiating sorcerer, indicating the response by the course it traversed among the symbols. These represented, in an extraordinary jumble, the most sacred objects of Christian and heathen worship, mingled with birds, beasts, and fishes, the sun and all the heavenly bodies, lakes and mountains, trees and rivers, men and women, and the houses, cities, and countries they inhabit.—(Sch. i. 426; see also Scheffer, *The History of Lapland*, 1704.)

NOTE 39.—*Songs and Incantations.*

Page 382.—The magical song in my poem is taken nearly verbatim from Mr. Schoolcraft's text (Sch. i. 398). It seems to have been the incantation actually used by the Meda Maiden on her first appearance as a *Jossakeed*, or prophetess. Far from being meaningless rhapsodies, or the utterances of an always sudden impulse, these magical songs are usually prepared compositions, often traditional and of remote antiquity, recorded by means of symbolic notation, and (where not original) learnt with much trouble, and frequently at heavy cost, by those admitted to the mystic societies.

Mr. Schoolcraft claims to have been first to inform the general public of the fact, well known to 'persons familiar with the state of the Western tribes,' that 'the songs of the Indian priesthood and Wabenoes were sung from a kind of pictorial notation [*kekeenowin*], made on bark.' 'The words of these songs are fixed, and not variable, as well as the notes to which they are sung.

But these words, to be repeated, must have been previously learned by, and known to, the singer' (Sch. i. 361),—the symbols (birds, beasts, men, etc.) do not generally represent words or sounds according to an accepted system, but serve to recall by association the details of each particular song. For example, the key-symbol representing 'a magic bone decorated with feathers—a symbol indicative of the power of passing through the air,' guides a person acquainted with that special chant to the corresponding verse—'The sky! the sky I sail upon!'—(Sch. i. 374.)

Of the hieroglyphical records referred to, a great number are transcribed by Mr. Schoolcraft from the original Ojibway, with English translations (evidently not always literal, though substantially accurate), and in several cases pictorial facsimiles are given, illustrative of the various forms of magic (Sch. i. 358-411).

The following chants, belonging to the mysteries of the 'higher Jeesukawin'—the sacred prophetic art—are compositions by the Meda Maiden herself. 'The subjoined specimens of her hieratic songs and hymns,' says Mr. Schoolcraft, 'are taken down verbatim. It is a peculiarity observed in this and other instances of the same kind, that the words of these chants are never repeated by the natives without the tune or air,—which was full of intonation, and uttered in so hollow and suspended, or inhaled, a voice, that it would require a practised composer to note it down. The chorus is not less peculiarly fixed, and some of its guttural tones are startling.'—(Sch. i. 397.)

HYMNS BY OGEEWYAHN OQUT OQUA.

1. 'CHANT TO THE DEITY (*embodying the response of the Deity invoked.*)

'I am the living body of the Great Spirit above,
(The Great Spirit, the Ever-living Spirit above,)
The living body of the Great Spirit,
(Whom all must heed).
"Heh! heh! heh! heh!"

(*Sharp and peculiar chorus, untranslatable.*)

'I am the Great Spirit of the sky,
The overshadowing power.
I illumine earth,
I illumine heaven.
"Way, ho! ho! ho! ho!"

(*Slow, hollow, peculiar chorus.*)

'Ah say! what Spirit, or Body, is this Body?
(That fills the world around,
Speak, man!) ah say!
What Spirit, or Body, is this Body?
"Way, ho! ho! ho! ho!"

(*Chorus as in the preceding, with voice and drum.*)'

2. 'HYMN TO THE SUN.

'The sky or day I tread upon, that makes a noise.
(I Ge-Zis—Maker of light.) (*Repeat four times.*)
"A! a! a! ha! aha!"

'The place where it sinks down—the maker of day.
When I was first ordained to be—(I Ge Zis.)
"A! a! a! ha! aha!"'

3. 'To the Great Spirit.

'Look thou at the Spirit.
It is he that is spoken of who stays our lives—
Who abides in the sky. (*Repeat four times.*)
"A! a! a! ha! aha!"' (Sch. i. 399-401.)

It is difficult to give satisfactory specimens of the Meda and Wabeno (higher and lower Magic) chants without the pictorial symbols which belong to each verse,—as an extract from a 'Synopsis of a Wabeno song' may serve to show. The relation of this synopsis to the fuller description preceding it will be gathered from the following detailed explanation of 'Key-symbol No. 1':—'Figure 1 depicts a preliminary chant. The figure represents a lodge prepared for a nocturnal dance [the *nocturnal* celebration specially characterises this baser form of magic], marked with seven crosses to denote dead bodies, and crowned with a magic bone and feathers. It is fancied that this lodge has the power of locomotion, or crawling about. The owner and inviter of the guests [the magician or "medicine-man"] sings solus:—

'Wa-be-no (*Wabeno-spirit*)
Pe mo da (*he creep,—Ind. mood*)
Ne we-ge-wam (*my lodge—"wigwam."*)
Hi au ha
Nhuy e way
Nhuy e way.
Ha! ha! huh! huh! huh!
My lodge crawls by the Wabeno's power.'

(Sch. i. 373.)

' SYNOPSIS OF WABENO SONG.

Chant or Incantation.	*Key-Symbol, or Ideographic Term of Notation.**
1. My lodge crawls by the Wabeno power.	1. A lodge for nocturnal dances.
2. Under the ground I have taken him.	2. A man holding a live snake.
3. I too am a Wabeno.	3. The figure of a man sitting, crowned with feathers [the Magician himself].
4. I make the Wabeno dance.	4. A man or spirit dancing on the half of the sky.
5. The sky! the sky I sail upon!	5. A magic bone, decorated with feathers.
6. I am a Wabeno spirit—this is my work.	6. A horned serpent [Gitchi Keenâbic, the symbol of life].
7. I work with two bodies.	7. A hunter with a bow and arrow [seeking power to see animals at a distance].
8. The owl! the owl! the great black owl!	8. An owl.
9. Let me hunt for it.	9. A wolf standing on the sky [the gift of vigilance is sought].
10. Burning flames—burning flames.	10. Flames.

* In some cases I have taken the reading of the fuller description.

11. My little child, I show you pity.	11. An unborn infant, with one wing.
12. I turn round in standing.	12. A tree—supposed to be animated by a demon.
13. Wabeno-power (occult).	13. A female figure. ("She is depicted as one who has rejected the addresses of many. A rejected lover [*i.e.* one who may be consulting the Magician to gain this spell] procures mystic medicine. . . . This causes her to sleep, during which he makes a captive of her and carries her off.")

(Sch. i. 380, 381; also see pp. 373-380.)

The foregoing—from a song of thirty-eight verses—will sufficiently illustrate the character and objects of the lower Indian magic. It is expressly stated by her biographer that my heroine, the noble Meda and Jossakeed Ogeewyahn-Oqut-Oqua, never debased herself by practising the Wabeno's nefarious necromantic arts.—(Sch. i. 394.)

Though unconnected with magic, the following specimen of an Ojibway war-song will hardly be out of place. It was sung, 'with its appropriate tune,' to Mr. Schoolcraft, in 1824, by Bwoinais, a gallant warrior of Lake Superior, who had used it during the then existing war with the Sioux or Dacotas.

'From the south—they come, the warlike birds—
Hark to their passing screams!
I wish for the body of the fiercest bird,
As swift—as cruel—as strong.

'I cast away my body to the chance of battle.
Full happy am I to lie on the field—
On the field over the enemy's line.'

'The sentiments of the following song,' writes Mr. Schoolcraft, 'were uttered by the celebrated WAUBOJEEG, as the leader of the Ojibways, after a victory over the combined Sioux and Sauks and Foxes, at the falls of St. Croix, during the latter part of the eighteenth century:*—

WAR-SONG OF WAUBOJEEG.

'Hear my voice, ye heroes!
On that day when our warriors sprang
With shouts on the dastardly foe,
Just vengeance my heart burned to take
On the cruel and treacherous breed,
The Bwoin †—the Fox—the Sauk.

'And here, on my breast, have I bled!
See—see—my battle-scars!
Ye mountains, tremble at my yell!
I strike for life.

* *Seventeenth* in text, through an evident misprint—see vol. i. 149. This is the Waubojeeg who was related to the seeress, Ogeewyahn Oqut Oqua (Sch. i. 390).

† The Sioux.

'But who are my foes? They shall die,
They shall fly o'er the plains like a fox;
They shall shake like a leaf in the storm.
Perfidious dogs! they roast our sons with fire!

'Five winters in hunting we'll pass,
While mourning our warriors slain,
Till our youth grown to men
For the battle-path trained,
Our days like our fathers we'll end.

'Ye are dead, noble men! ye are gone—
My brother—my fellow—my friend!
On the death-path where brave men must go:
But we live to revenge you! We haste
To die as our forefathers died.' (Sch. ii. 60-62.)

NOTE 40.—*Kekeenowin.*

Page 417.—'Kekeenowin [Pictorial Records] or *Hieratic signs* of the Medawin and Jeesukawin. This class of signs is devoted to the forest priesthood.' . . . 'For their pictographic devices the Ojibway Indians have two terms, namely, *Ke-keé-win*, or such things as are generally understood by the tribe; and *Ke-kee-no-win*, or teachings of the Medas or priests, and Josakeeds or prophets. The knowledge of the latter is chiefly confined to persons who are versed in their system of magic medicine, or their religion, and may be deemed hieratic. The former consists of the common figurative signs, such as are employed at places of sepulture, or by hunting and travelling parties.* It is also employed in the *Muzzinâbiks,* or rock-writings. Many of the figures are common to both, and are seen in the drawings generally; but this results from the figure-alphabet being precisely the same in both, while the devices of the *Nugamoons,* or medicine, Wabeno, hunting, and war-songs, are known only to the initiates who have learned them.

'The subjects to which the North American Indian applies his pictographic skill may be regarded as follows, namely:—

1. KEKEEWIN.

A.	————— . .	Travelling, etc.
B.	Adjidâtigwun	Sepulture.

2. KEKEENOWIN.

C.	Medâwin	Medicine.
D.	Minor Jeesukâwin . .	Necromancy.
E.	Wâbeno	Revelry.
F.	Keossâwin	Hunting.
G.	Higher Jeesukâwin . .	Prophecy
H.	Nundobewunewun . .	War.
I.	Sageâwin	Love.
K.	Muzzinâbikon . .	History.'

(Sch. i. 351, 352.)

* When travelling in the Rocky Mountains in 1859, I found this hieroglyphic system superseded, for common purposes, by certain syllabic signs invented for the Cree Indians by an English missionary. They were then in use among the Mountain Assiniboines, and are now no doubt employed by the Ojibways, whose language is akin to that of the Crees. The half-civilised Cherokees have long had signs of a similar nature. (See *Saskatchewan*, p. 149, and Plates, p. 424.)

'Pictorial devices which refer to the Jeesukawin have been less easily accessible than any other branch. There is a feeling of sacredness and secrecy connected with them, which prevents their being revealed even to the uninitiated Indians. It is the only branch of their art of picture-writing which is withheld from common [that is, comparatively common] use. Signs of the Medawin and the Wabeno,—of hunting, sepulture, war, and other objects, are more or less known to all, and are accessible to all, who are admitted to the secret societies. But the prophetic art exists by itself. It is exclusive, peculiar, personally experimental.'—(Sch. i. 390.) 'The prophet begins to try his power in secret. . . . As he goes on, he puts down the figures of his dreams or revelations, by symbols, on bark or other material . . . and he thus has a record of his principal revelations. If what he predicts is verified . . . the record is appealed to as proof of his prophetic power and skill. Time increases his fame. His *kekeewins*, or records, are finally shown to the old people, who meet together and consult upon them, for the whole nation believe in these revelations. They in the end give their approval, and declare that he is gifted as a prophet—is inspired with wisdom, and is fit to lead the opinions of the nation.' (Statement by Chingwauk, a principal chief, and well-known Indian priest or Meda, at Michillimackinac, in 1839.)—(Sch. i. 112, 114.)

THE END.

EDINBURGH UNIVERSITY PRESS :

THOMAS AND ARCHIBALD CONSTABLE, PRINTERS TO HER MAJESTY.